HIMALAYAN HEARTBEAT
By KEN ANDERSON

Published by
CHRISTIAN BLIND MISSION INTERNATIONAL
AFFILIATED WITH
CHRISTOFFEL-BLINDENMISSION

HIMALAYAN HEARTBEAT

By KEN ANDERSON

TWENTIETH CENTURY STEWARDSHIP IN FIRST CENTURY DIMENSIONS!

Discover the penetrating witness of a wealthy young engineer who dedicated his life . . . and his fortune . . . to the lowly people of India's Himalayan foothills. This is more than the story of a missionary doctor . . . it's the dramatic unfolding of a concept of Christian giving that reaches across the centuries to the first New Testament Church for its pattern. HIMALAYAN HEARTBEAT is the true-life portrait of Dr. Geoffrey Lehmann, a modern missionary medic.

HIMALAYAN HEARTBEAT

by Ken Anderson

*Discover the penetrating Witness of a
wealthy Young Engineer who Dedicated His
Life . . . and His Fortune . . . to the Lowly
People of India's Himalayan foothills.*

TWENTIETH CENTURY STEWARDSHIP IN FIRST CENTURY DIMENSIONS!

Published by
CHRISTIAN BLIND MISSION INTERNATIONAL
AFFILIATED WITH
CHRISTOFFEL-BLINDENMISSION

PREFACE

It was with immense pleasure that I received the invitation from CBMI — Christian Blind Mission International, a division of Christoffel-Blindenmission, West Germany, to write the preface to the second edition of HIMALAYAN HEARTBEAT. It is through the kindness of CBMI that we have the opportunity to read something of the on-going faithfulness of God in sustaining the vision and ministry of Geoffrey and Monica Lehmann, and Herbertpur Christian Hospital, during the last decade since the first edition.

In 1982 Dr Lehmann had the privilege of visiting the CBMI headquarters in Bensheim and he spoke enthusiastically, on his return to India, of his time with the team there and how much he had appreciated the knowledgeable interest of Pastor Wiesinger in the ministry at Herbertpur. During the 1970's and 1980's CBMI has been the major funding agency subsidising the eye care programe, both at the hospital and in the eye camps. Their generosity has extended to new staff quarters for the ophthalmologist and four of his team, instruments, operating theatre furniture, portable generator and a steady flow of funds to support eye department staff, medicines and other supplies. CBMI has also approved a major grant for the construction of an eye unit and this exciting prospect is being taken up as the size and scope of the work develops. It has been particularly gratifying to see the on-going involvement, hand in hand with the changes. Pastor Wiesinger and his associates share the Lehmanns' concern for the continuing acute need of eye care in rural and hilly areas around Herbertpur.

In 1973 the hospital was passed over to the Emmanuel Hospital Association, an Indian Christian medical mission, and in December 1978, Dr. Lehmann retired from all clinical work. Since 1982, Dr. Sydney Thyle, previously lecturer in ophthalmology at the Christian Medical College, Ludhiana, has joined the team and is heading up the work of the eye department.

Truly the name Dr. Geoffrey D. Lehmann shall be remembered for decades as one of evangelical Christianity's most unusual philanthropists. He and his beloved Monica combined love and skill and many years to touch the lives of multitudes. On such a foundation, the ministry of Herbertpur Christian Hospital moves forward.

The story of the Lehmanns' continues to unfold as in 1983 they thanked God for His love and grace in the 50 years of their marriage and they look forward to 1986, the 50th anniversary of the start of the work at Herbertpur.

HIMALAYAN HEARTBEAT has found it's way to the four corners of the world, both in English and German (through the kindness of CBMI) and the Lehmanns' have received many letters, including one from behind the Iron Curtain, of how the Lord has spoken to people through this book calling them to the mission field.

I am delighted to have the privilege of commending the second edition with its on-going testimony to the God who never fails.

Paul East, Administrator
Herbertpur Christian Hospital
Dist. Dehra Dun, (U.P.) India

FOREWORD

I recall a classroom journalism lecture by a well-known author who had been a prisoner of war in Europe. A novel burned in his heart, so obsessing him that he saved candy wrappers received from the Red Cross, and wrote his book in fine print on these scraps of paper.

Another lecturer told of a life so busy, yet a literary compulsion so demanding, he devoted ten to twenty minutes each day to a handwritten manuscript as he sat at lunch.

This book has come into being under similar circumstances.

Many chapters were written while traveling, a typewriter on my lap or a dictation machine at my side. In motel rooms, during snatched moments at home, amid lulls in the normal flow of activity, page by page the story has come into print.

So strong has been the compulsion of my heart to make known the Herbertpur experience.

I am grateful to Dr. and Mrs. Lehmann for their cooperation and their confidence. These are quality people, who not only do not seek publicitiy but rather shy from it. Only when persuaded of the value in an enlarged outreach for their testimony did they agree to such exposure.

I commend and extend my gratitude to Christian Blind Mission International for their vision in making possible this large and special edition of the book.

It is my prayer that the Lord of the Harvest, whom Dr. and Mrs. Geoffrey Lehmann have served so faithfully, will use this instrument as a spiritual tool to discipline and direct those who seek spiritual meaning in their lives.

The motivations which have come to my own life confirm this conviction!

KEN ANDERSON
720 N. Lake Street
Warsaw, Indiana
July 1985

1 You have no doubt had it happen.
A stranger.
Name.
Face.
Background and occupation.
Completely unknown.

Then, as though on cue, the stranger steps out of the wings to appear prominently in the drama of your life.

So it was with me in the case of one Geoffrey D. Lehmann.

I had been in northernmost Pakistan, with Heinz Fussle, Swiss cinematographer, on location for the production of a film at Bach Memorial Hospital just outside colorful Abbottabad in the gauntly picturesque Himalayan foothills. Were it not for strife among men and nations, and had I been disposed to do so, I could have followed those foothills southward through beautiful Kashmir and on into India to another hospital.

This hospital I was to reach . . . indeed to discover the existence of . . . not by means of terrestrial thoroughfares but across the route of strange circumstance.

We had overstayed our schedule, as sullen skies prolonged efforts to complete exterior photography for *The Harvester*, color motion picture on which we were working. One sequence, normally an afternoon of shooting, took nearly five days to complete.

Arrangements had been made for a homeward side trip to Mussoorie, high in the Indian Himalayas to the north of New Delhi, for exploratory discussion with Alan Norrish, head of a British mission.

As day after day brought no substantial break in the skies, however, I wrote to him, suggesting we meet in New Delhi.

When we at last marked out the final scene of the script, and could make plans for the long jet homeward, I sent off a wire to Mussoorie, giving my arrival time in New Delhi.

Mr. Norrish was there to meet me.

"I'm terribly sorry," he said, "but I only have a couple of hours. Something has come up and I will need to get back to Mussoorie as quickly as possible."

As politely as I could, I told him it was not possible to plan an entire film in two hours, which led him to inquire, "Is there no chance at all that you could come with me?"

Not waiting for a reply, he added with wry cordiality, "As you know, we Englishmen find it difficult to understand how you Americans can pace yourselves the way you do."

"I've got to be back in the States by the end of the week," I told him, "and I need to make a couple of stops en route."

He looked at his watch. "I really can't stay on," he said. "It's quite impossible. We received word that the Dalai Lama is coming to Mussoorie tomorrow, and I must be there. There is a good deal of work being done among Tibetan refugees in the hills, and we are all anxious to keep the best possible relations with the Dalai Lama and his government."

The Dalai Lama!

Since boyhood, Tibet had fascinated me. I was raised by my maternal grandmother, a great intercessor for the cause of missions, who took the dirge out of many a winter's night with tales of harvestland heroism. One of her favorite subjects was the Tibetan frontier.

"There would be a rather good opportunity for you to meet the Dalai Lama," Mr. Norrish continued, "if you thought you could take the time."

Within moments, we were at the airline ticket counter, cancelling all of my stop-overs between New Delhi and Chicago!

2 Sleeper space was sold out on the train to Dehra Dun, and Mr. Norrish advised against travel by coach. Train travel is the norm for India, and coach compartments, designed to accompany eight or perhaps ten passengers, frequently pull out of the station with twice that many ticket holders massed into each little section.

A missionary wife told me of traveling half-way across India in this manner, she and her four children tight against the windows with some fifteen men sharing the compartment. When the inevitable happened, and two of the children asked to go to the washroom, the men obligingly hoisted them above their heads, and moved them hand over hand to the door, returning them in the same manner a few moments later.

"We could go by taxi," Mr. Norrish said.

I cringed, for our organization departs rather abruptly from what might be called Hollywood-type film budgets, and no accomodation is ever given to such luxuries as a trip of one hundred and fifty miles by taxi.

Mr. Norrish explained that, were we to take the train to Dehra Dun, it still would be necessary to hire a cab for the additional twenty miles up the mountain. And while we could not travel to Dehra Dun as cheaply as we might have by sleeper car, we could go all the way to Mussoorie, hold the taxi for a day and a night, and I could then return to New Delhi to make my plane connections. All of this would cost no more than a round trip ticket by air, were such service available.

So we made quick work of hiring a cab, taking care to make sure the driver and his vehicle would be trustworthy. For India, one of earth's developing nations, has had to learn the art of total salvage. Automobiles, long beyond the age of usability by American standards, bring a good price when offered for sale. "First class taxi!" a driver exudes, as he tries to usher you into a jalopy that seems utterly incapable of negotiating another mile.

The driver of the cab we selected was a handsome young Sikh, and one look at him reminded me that Sikhs can be found in so many parts of Asia, serving as building and shop guards, often in situations where personal integrity is of utmost importance. The car itself was a new *Hindustan*, Indian built and in both design and performance a tribute to the national growth envisioned by Mahatma Ghandi and implemented by Jawaharlal Nehru.

It was by now the very last of April, and already New Delhi had begun to feel the thermal blazes that rise up from the sun-scorched plains of central India. So, as we drove out of the city at evening fall, one felt a sense of relief to know we would be heading upward toward the eternal cool of the world's highest mountains.

One does not travel quickly across the highways of India, even the best highways.

The motor vehicle serves only a fractional minority of those who travel. Bullock carts, bicycles, and throngs of people afoot monopolize the highways.

The brake, the horn, and then the accelerator, in that order, comprise an automobile's three most important functions.

During the journey's first hour, Mr. Norrish and I discussed preliminary aspects of what was to become *India Today*, a motion picture visualizing the growth of India and the worth of its youth. But as evening fell, bringing with it the intrigue of India at night, I found it increasingly difficult to keep my mind on anything but the sights outside each window. We traveled more as a car in a procession than a vehicle on a trip, due to the heavy, plodding traffic, and so one could view the countryside with more than casual glimpses.

Mr. Norrish, perhaps remembering his first encounter with sights along the Indian road, not only left me to my gazing, but regularly answered questions and pointed out objects of interest which otherwise would surely have escaped my observation.

In actuality, this was my second visit to India. My first, several years before, had been limited to entry by way of Madras in the far south, a flight from Madras to Bombay, and then airborne exit from Bombay homeward.

The cities of India are interesting, to be sure, but they are at best like the attractive covers of a book. The pages of the book, depicting the real people and their life, are to be found by perusing the countryside.

If I may extend the metaphor, this motor trip by night, and the one returning to New Delhi which was to follow by day, comprised my homework ordained of God to prepare my heart for the searching glimpses He was to give me of this great land and its opportunities for dedicated service.

It is such a quantitative experience, seeing India, and one's first glimpses are to the eye like the meaningless chatter of a new language before one has at least begun to distinguish familiar words and phrases. But the impact was there, the intrigue and emotional tug and the growing sense of so many one would like to befriend and help.

I especially remember the villages at almost every turn of the road. Indian farmers live communal style, together with a few shopkeepers and artisans. Far into the night, I saw sewing machines at work, entire families engaged in the manufacture of shoes, smiths at their fires as they fashioned crude plowshares to turn the soil.

One of the most common expressions in India is, "Will you have a cup of tea?" Every little village has two, three or more tea shops, where for a couple of annas one may drink a cup of fresh brewed tea. The Hindu rarely drinks alcoholic beverages in public, and so the little tea shops serve as a rather refreshing exception to the drinking establishments one normally expects to find.

Just before midnight, we came upon a brilliantly lighted village. People thronged the road, and as our Sikh slowed his cab to the pace of the foot traffic, Mr. Norrish, who had been dozing momentarily, sat up.

"It almost looks like a *mela*," he said.

I asked, "What's a *mela*?"

"It might compare to what you commonly call the county fair in the States," he told me.

"They exhibit livestock and produce?" I asked, remembering the Pakistani version of a midwest farmer's sale barn.

"A *mela* is not that kind of fair," Mr. Norrish explained. "It is actually a religious festival."

"What we have here," our driver said in characteristic idiom, "is a Hindu wedding." He rolled the corners of his beard in a gesture as much the trademark of the Sikh as his long, turban-wrapped hair.

"So it is," Mr. Norrish observed.

"Must be someone quite wealthy," I said.

Mr. Norrish sighed. "It could be quite the contrary. These people will sometimes mortgage everything they have, put themselves into debt for many years, just so they can put on this kind of show at the time of a child's wedding."

He thought for a moment, then added, "It wouldn't be so bad, if the wedding were a time of happiness, as we've come to know it in the Western world, but all too often this is not the case. For many a young bride, it is the most frightful event of her life."

I sensed the hurt in his voice, the yearning of a man who desired so intensely and had tried so long to bring the people of this great country into the kind of living concepts which have made life so completely different in what ethnologists would call the "Christian World."

In the face of a bursting population explosion, India continues to propagate large families. Sex is an object of worship, sometimes so sordid as to turn the head of the most calloused Western visitor. I know of at least one temple wholly given to the priestly

7

contemplation of new techniques for the pursuit of sensual pleasure.

While some of the ancient writings counsel husbands to seek happiness for their wives — and there are, of course, happy marriages — too often the Indian male has little thought of affection and romance in relation to the connubial state.

We came directly alongside the hub of festivities. It was undeniably colorful, people dressed in their finest. Beautiful fabrics festooned the enclosure, arching up like a kind of covering over the honored guests.

As we moved past, I watched from the back window of the cab until we had gone completely out of sight. It was so far . . . it was thousands of miles and hundreds of years . . . it was eternity . . . the gulf between me and my kind of life and the cultural and spiritual momentums which had brought these people to their wedding feast.

And yet I knew I must be honest.

What of America's divorce mills and overcrowded marriage counselling rooms? An artist in Singapore, engaged in making theater billboards, once told me, "When we get an American film to illustrate, my boss instructs me to play up the sex." Was there any basic difference between the Western male, who made ecclesiastical pilgrimages at Christmas and Easter and on occasional Sundays, but lived in a constant moral hypocrisy, and the Hindu man with his ten million gods and his base desires?

I thought of Jerusalem — Golgotha, rising skull-like above the Garden Tomb at the gates of the City. Atop Golgotha, like the remembrance of the sin that was atoned for there, sprawls a Mohammedan cemetery. Onward to the East lie the nations of Islam, India and the vast Buddhist dominions. And to the West, toward the land of my birth, those nations to whom the torch of the Gospel was carried while others waited and yet wait in darkness.

My heart was being prepared to evaluate with new respect those who have come from the Light to pass beyond Golgotha into the vast darkness.

3 Morning lay just beyond the darkness, as we began the winding ascent from Dehra Dun to Mussoorie. One could see nothing of the mountains, only the road ahead, but on two occasions full grown panthers loped gracefully along the sideway to give a continuing touch of India to the last of our journey.

Morning's first touch illuminated our entry into Mussoorie, giving it a Disneyland silhouette against the pale sky. An occasional dog barked. Here and there a window light flickered. But the city itself lay silent. Stark contrast to my first glimpses of India and, indeed, to the hive-like excitement which the full of morning would bring to these streets.

Our taxi took us as far as vehicles were permitted to go. Then, reaffirming arrangements with our Sikh to await my return journey some twenty-eight hours later, we set out on foot up the trail to Edgehill, to the headquarters compound of Alan Norrish's mission.

Though half-bewildered by weariness, I could not sleep.

I lay in my bed, listening to the morning songs of the birds and the rising din of human activity, and thinking how profound it was to be in the great and endless drama that is called India.

Pakistan had held its fascinations, to be sure, but the Pakistanis are Muslims, almost to the last man, rabid in their conviction that there is but one God. You can talk with a Pakistani about Moses and Abraham and David. They consider Jesus one of the great prophets.

But in those villages, through which we had come during the night, lived innumerable multitudes who had never heard of Bethlehem or Nazareth, and a hill on which once stood three crosses whose shadows fell so far toward the West.

After a bit of tossing, I arose and dressed, and selected a meandering trail up from Edgehill to the famous Mussoorie Ridge. By the time I reached the summit, the sun had risen full, flooding with light the awesome spectacle of the eternal Himalayan snows. Immense peaks, rising to heights of over twenty-six thousand feet, and then on and on ever higher toward Nepal and the crest of Mount Everest.

Where in all the world can the human eye behold a more wondrous vantage? It is beyond the vocabulary of audible description.

Yet, even as I looked, I remembered the things my grandmother had told me. The forbidden mountain passes, shutting out Tibet from the rest of the world. White majesty containing a kingdom of darkness. How strange it is, the world God made and the world man then defiled.

At midmorning, Alan Norrish and I made our way down the steep incline to Wynberg-Allen Schools. I had not heard of this institution before, but at first sight of the campus I could understand why even a conservative Englishman used superlatives to speak of it as one of the most significant private schools in all of India. It had been conceived in the minds and hearts of British residents back in the days of colonial empire, as a school for children of the neglected Anglo-Indian community. Today, while one yet finds many Anglo-Indians, the student body also includes those who are fully Indian in heritage as well as students from such nations as Ceylon, Thailand and Tibet.

It was those students from Tibet who occupied our attention this day.

Almost an exact four years had passed since the Dalai Lama, in his flight from the bloody Chinese Communist overrun of Tibet, sought refuge in Mussoorie.

Disguised as a Tibetan soldier, he had walked out of the Potala, seat of the government and religion of Tibet in the capital city of Lhasa. He had crossed the Che-la, towering mountain pass just beyond the city, had crossed the turbulent Thang-bo river, which swirls its way through the Himalayas to become the sacred Brahmaputra of India. On and on, by foot and on horseback, until he reached a monastery, high in the Yarto-tag-la range, hoping here to set up negotiations with the Chinese.

Then word came of the bombardment of the Potala in Lhasa, as the invaders slaughtered multitudes of monks, carefully examining each to see if they might have destroyed the Dalai Lama and thus broken the will to live in the hearts of every Tibetan.

Tibetans believe the Dalai Lama to be the reincarnation of the god Chenrezi, although

11

the Dalai Lama is said to have questioned whether or not he really is divinity, and so, to keep alive the spirit of Tibet he must escape to India. There he could seek to negotiate the all but hopeless hope of winning back Tibet's freedom from the Communist invaders.

From Mussoorie, the Dalai Lama had subsequently gone on to Dharmsala to the northwest in the India Himalayas, and it was from Dharmsala where he was coming this day in late April of 1963, for the purpose of visiting the many Tibetan refugees in Mussoorie, but expressly to observe the progress of those of his young people attending Wynberg-Allen Schools.

It was the Dalai Lama, and the strange events spawning his interest in Wynberg-Allen Schools, which was to bring about my meeting with Dr. Geoffrey D. Lehmann.

4 While this is not intended to be a treatise on the Tibetans, but rather a look at the country people of India through the heart of a truly great man, this man . . . this Dr. Geoffrey Lehmann, whom I was soon to meet . . . shares with many alert Christians a deep concern for Tibetans. And, as I have stated, it was our mutual affinity toward the Tibetan situation which was to cause our encounter.

To most of the world, Tibet is the real Shangri-la, a fantasy kingdom high against the sky. Occasional westerners have penetrated its borders, mostly through China, perhaps no more than a half dozen allowed as far as Lhasa. On the underside, against

India, missionaries have made virtually no contact, except with nomads and traders who ventured down across the border.

In the disputed borderlands beyond Kansu province, in northwest China, missionaries have made more frequent contact with Tibetans. Some even established residence in Tibetan communities. But wherever missionaries have encountered Tibetans, few conversions have resulted, so firmly enmeshed is Buddhist doctrine and philosophy and culture with every detail of Tibetan life. The Dalai Lama, as both temporal and spiritual head, and the tens of thousands of lamas and monks as his subsidiaries, ruled the country as a completely religious state.

In 1948, while on a film assignment across the mainland of China, I had an appointment to meet the Panchan Lama, second most important among the human deities of Tibet, but the appointment had to be cancelled due to heavy fighting between Chinese Communist and Nationalist troops in the northwest provinces. I did, however, spend some time with missionaries who had come down from Sian, prominent missionary outpost in the area.

One of them told me his mission had worked among the Tibetans for almost forty years without so much as one professed convert. Some secret believers, perhaps, but none who dared to overtly identify himself as a follower of Christ.

Tibet not only rejected Christianity but also closed its borders to western culture and commerce, except for yak caravans, plodding across the lower mountain passes into China, India and Kashmir for the purpose of carrying on outer world commerce in the simple commodities of life. Tibet made no gesture to share its vast potential with the rest of mankind.

"We are a people who find contentment in religion and philosophy," a government spokesman once told me. "We have no need for the luxuries that betray the mind from seeking after truth."

For many years, small groups of Christians have prayed that a door might be opened to Tibet, a doorway to opportunity for the presentation of the Gospel.

Such a door remained fast shut.

Then came the invasion of Chinese Communists, greedy for the vast mineral wealth latent in the towering Tibetan strata. Instead of a doorway to Tibet, a doorway of opportunity for the Gospel, there came to be a doorway from Tibet, a doorway of unprecedented spiritual opportunity.

As news of the Dalai Lama's flight into India spread among the six million inhabitants of Tibet, throngs of them escaped into India before Communists could close off trade routes. The refugees include many of Tibet's prominent citizens, those of the nobility for whom, whatever their measure of courage, remaining in Tibet meant almost certain death.

Once established in Dharmsala, the Dalai Lama set up a government in exile, bringing together his prime minister, cabinet and prominent religious leaders.

From the outset, the Dalai Lama showed warm interest in missionaries. He requested copies of the Bible in order that he might study what he called "the prophecies of Jesus." He took note, with the passing of

14

time, that many of those who had opened arms of welcome, when he first arrived in India, grew lax in their concern. The Christians, however, remained the same, their concern as radiant after the first year of exile as it had been on the first day.

While Christians expressed and demonstrated genuine concern for the physical needs of refugee Tibetans, they avoided the hypocrisy of any form of spiritual trickery and, instead, made quite clear their wish for thinking Tibetans to evaluate the Christian faith.

When the Dalai Lama began expressing concern that the children of Tibetan parents be given an opportunity for Western education, the warmth he had found in the hearts of missionaries and national Christians made it almost a matter of course to look for schools operated by evangelicals.

At the outset, some fifty of Tibet's finest youth, each destined to play a significant role in the nation's future, were personally chosen by the Dalai Lama and instructed to enroll at Wynberg-Allen.

"Your Highness," school officials said, "we take great care not to force the Christian faith on anyone. It is a personal matter between the individual and God. But we do carefully present the teachings of the Bible to our students. As a result, many of them become Christians."

The Dalai Lama was quiet for a moment, then said, "We have a new constitution, and our constitution does not prevent a Tibetan from becoming a Christian."

This is not to say that multitudes of Tibetan young people have embraced Christianity. Very few have done so, so deeply embedded are Buddhist influences from earliest child-

15

hood. In fact, some have expressed restlessness, even subdued rebellion, in the face of Christian teaching. And, if the spiritual apathy of the Christian church continues, with so few expressing prayerful concern for the situation of the Tibetans, it is unlikely there will be any sizeable turning to the true God.

I have sat for an hour at a time, watching one of the teaching lamas lead small children in memorization sessions. They commit to memory vast portions of the Buddhist scripture, and children, at an early age, can quote scripture for hours at a time and answer mature questions on doctrine.

No casual encounter with the Christian message is likely to bring them to a quick conversion.

But the fact of opportunity remains, and so it was with much deliberation that officials of Wynberg-Allen Schools prepared for the visit of the Dalai Lama. His visit, in essence for the purpose of expressing gratitude, would inevitably have the larger motivation of observing the attitudes of Tibetan students toward Wynberg-Allen.

I could sense the air of expectancy and tension, as Mr. Norrish and I stepped into the school campus.

An extended greeting line had been formed, first the Tibetan students, then the other students, and after that missionaries, faculty members, and special guests. We were placed at the farthest end of the line, near to the entrance of Windy Ridge, the faculty residence selected as the site for a special tea to be given the distinguished visitor and his entourage.

The waiting line came to orderly attention, as the appointed time neared for the Dalai

Lama's arrival.

The time came and passed, and the crowd grew restless.

I noticed one man, whom I took at first glance to be either an Australian or an Englishman, moving among the people. Because so many sought to question him, my first surmisal was that he must be the headmaster at the school. He had the brisk manner of one who finds it difficult to excuse the absence of either organization or punctuality.

As he neared the last of the line, in a bright Oxford accent I heard him say, "The Dalai Lama has been delayed at a meeting with the Tibetans, but we have been assured he will be on his way shortly."

Then, as he approached us, he saw Mr. Norrish, smiled warmly and said, "Ah, Alan, so good you could be here! I understood you had made a business trip down to Delhi."

"So I did," Mr. Norrish told him. Then he turned to me and said, "I'd like you to meet the gentleman I was to see in Delhi. I persuaded him to return with me, so we could talk business while we were traveling."

He then gave my name, introducing me to Dr. Geoffrey D. Lehmann.

"Dr. Lehmann is chairman of the Board of Governors here at Wynberg-Allen, " he added.

"Aren't you the gentleman from America who makes religious films?" I was asked. My assent brought from him the further statement, "Then you must make a film for us here at Wynberg-Allen. When might it be possible to start such a project?"

I did not answer for two reasons. First, we are constantly meeting people who, on the spur of the moment, seem ready to engage us immediately in the production of a motion picture but, in reality, have no idea of what would be involved in such a project. Second, I did not give answer because the man whose name I had so quickly forgotten hurried on his way to take care of further details related to the occasion.

I did turn to Alan Norrish, and ask. "This gentleman is on the staff here at Wynberg-Allen?"

"Dr. Lehmann is Wynberg-Allen," Mr. Norrish replied. There was enough of a twinkle in his eye to suggest I should ask more about this man before dismissing him from my mind.

Apparently Mr. Norrish expected as much, for he said, "Dr. Lehmann, apart from serving as chairman of the Board of Governors, is not on the regular staff here, nor does he reside in Mussoorie. I presume from your question you are not familiar with the work of the hospital down in Herbertpur. One of the most unique examples of Christian stewardship anywhere in the world today."

News spread through the crowd that the Dalai Lama was but a short distance away, and so we came quietly to attention, watching.

The Dalai Lama did not come just then, but the interim served to focus my attention once again on the Tibetan students down the line from where we stood.

Suppose we were to do a film about a young Tibetan, I mused, a refugee from Tibet who comes to Wynberg-Allen, hears the Christian message for the first time, and . . .

Just then, Geoffrey Lehmann returned.

"Have you given any further thought to the possibility of a film?" he asked me.

I said, "We might be quite interested in a

film story of the school, if it in some way involved these young Tibetans."

"Splendid!" he interrupted. "How much would such a film cost?"

"To do a short feature in black and white —" I began.

"Oh," he exclaimed, "but we must have color!"

So I quoted our basic budget for color, and then watched, momentarily amused, as he stood thinking. I supposed, as had so often been the case before, economic reality would now have its customary due.

Quite to my surprise, he looked up at me and said, "Let's do it! How soon could you begin?"

When, in a moment, he stepped away once more, I turned to Mr. Norrish and frankly asked, "This . . . this gentleman . . . is he just an enthusiast . . . a visionary?"

"When he said to you 'let's do it,'" Mr. Norrish told me, "it was like putting his name on a contract. Dr. Lehmann is a man of highest integrity. His word is his bond."

"He's the head of the mission out here . . . such as yourself?"

"He's the head of the hospital."

"The hospital?" I had so soon forgotten.

"At Herbertpur. It's quite a story. You see, Dr. Lehmann is a man of considerable means, and he with his wife have been independent missionaries here in India for some three decades. It's a thrilling story. I hope you have a chance to look into it sometime."

Within the half hour, the Dalai Lama and his party arrived. We were given a chance to meet His Highness personally. Then school faculty and staff members, together with a few guests such as myself, entered Windy Ridge for tea. I was placed next to the Dalai Lama's sister, a woman of charm and poise. The Dalai Lama, slightly elevated on an upholstered chair over which a maroon blanket had been placed as regal covering, presented a most interesting sight.

But my eyes kept drifting to the doctor from the place called Herbertpur. Not only because of his stated willingness to finance what I believed to be potentially a most unusual motion picture, but because, quite unknown to him or anyone else in the whole land of India, I had been a long time searching for some tangible definitions of Christian stewardship in a day when so many of God's children recognize Him only in the provision of the comforts they so lavishly bestow upon themselves.

Could it be God had providentially guided my way to Mussoorie, not for the fulfillment of a tourist's dream to meet someone such as the Dalai Lama but, eminently more meaningful, to encounter the living witness of a truly good steward? To discover, from his witness, answers long sought in my own quest for spiritual fulfillment, concepts, and principles of discipleship I might then share with others?

5 In November, when the heat had gone from the Jamuna bottom lands, I returned to India, to lay plans for the proposed film and, though I had not divulged this intent to the good doctor, to watch him at work and to search out his motives and to learn all I could of his past, in an effort to determine whether or not this might not be, as I strongly suspected, one of the notable examples of obedience and stewardship in the constituency of the contemporary church.

Our son, Max, and I had been in Europe during the month of August, working on *The Accuser*, a dramatic film designed for evangelism among the youth of Europe. The Lehmanns were in England on a holiday at the time, and so the two of us arranged to meet them in suburban Croydon, a half-hour train run from the heart of London.

Mrs. Lehmann had not been at Mussoorie during the time of the Dalai Lama's visit, but she was in Croydon, and the day spent with the two of them had added considerably to my anticipation that morning as our train chugged into Dehra Dun.

I had done badly on the train.

First of all, no one told me a passenger must bring his own bedding or rent a bed roll when traveling by sleeper. Nor did I realize the sleeper compartments, each with four uncurtained beds, tend to be coeducational!

A thoughtful student in my compartment shared one of his blankets, I used my briefcase as a pillow, but somehow I never did feel at ease sharing the compartment with a young Indian and his wife, even though their propriety was beyond reproach.

Then, very early in the morning, when I began to catch only the first bit of sleep, loud banging on our compartment door announced the availability of tea, in the partaking of which I could hardly have been less interested.

But as I stepped from the train, to find the

Lehmanns awaiting me, I sensed what I had felt many times. The faraway, strange loneliness of a country and culture so different from my own, and yet a sense of the familiar in the cordial presence of those to whom the surroundings were once as strange as they were now to me.

During the brief visit in Croydon, I had apparently mentioned my Scandinavian pedigree, all of my ancestors, to the best of my knowledge, having lived in the European northlands. In any case, standing with the Lehmanns on the Dehra Dun station platform was a Swedish missionary nurse, a near relative of the former heavyweight boxing champion from Sweden, and a woman abundantly gifted with spiritual radiance and personal charm.

I do not speak Swedish, apart from a sparse supply of words and phrases remembered from the Scandinavian community in northwest Iowa where I spent my childhood, but the woman spoke excellent English, and our conversation together with the Lehmanns served once again to forcibly remind me how often I find missionaries to be people who have discovered the center of their lives, and who do not need pretense and false imagery and materialistic externals to give meaning to their existence.

The Lehmanns had even arranged breakfast at a restaurant called the Indiana, that being the state of my residence back in America.

I particularly remember Mrs. Lehmann's warm concern as, in what appeared to me to be excellent use of the Hindustani tongue, she made sure the waiter understood my wishes perfectly, and the food, when delivered, was both clean and properly prepared.

Mrs. Lehmann ... her name is Monica except on occasions when, for some reason, her husband calls her Betty ... had been somewhat aloof during our visit in England. I did not mind, since I have often found the British slow to take a new American into friendship. Having so often been embarrassed by the conduct of the typical American tourist overseas, I don't blame them.

Here at Dehra Dun, however, I was like an old and well remembered friend.

The England visit had not been without its amenities, however, as was quickly evidenced when the doctor's wife asked if I might like some juice with my breakfast.

She looked fully into my eyes, just for a moment, as the wry evidence of a grin came to her face, and then as quickly went away. "They have to-may-to juice" she said, pronouncing each phrase distinctly.

We had had tomato juice in Croydon and, in her response as to whether or not I would like a second glass of what she called "to-mah-toe" juice, I had dared to foray a bit freely onto the beachhead of friendship by suggesting I would accept this, if that was all she had to offer, but would much prefer a glass of "to-may-toe" juice.

Breakfast over, the Lehmanns had shopping to attend to, for which they apologized, explaining that Herbertpur lies some twenty-five miles from Dehra Dun, and no-one can trek to the little city, for whatever reason, without thinking of multiple objectives.

No explanation would have been necessary, however. I had long ago learned to enjoy an Oriental bazaar. They are sight and sound and smell and experience unique unto themselves, with many little shops and hawkers and produce stands, and the endless moving of the human tide.

But the bazaar in Dehra Dun revealed something I had neither known nor expected.

The foreigner, coming from the western world into a developing country such as India, has a tendency to observe such things as a bazaar with a condescending eye. I had been guilty of such misconduct, although it is my determination to see all underprivileged peoples in the perspective of their potential rather than their present.

In the observance of bazaars, I have often thought of the American supermarket, with its over-abundance of everything. That morning, we purchased fruit and eggs, meat and flour and a few pounds of precious rationed sugar. In the same bazaar, however, the doctor was also able to secure vaccines kept in accordance with precise medical standards. He purchased bandages, disinfectant, and antiseptics. Then, to my complete amazement, he parked the hospital Land Rover in front of a most motley appearing establishment where, I supposed, one might pick up some kind of crude apparatus, perhaps a hoe for the garden, a hinge, or a window glass, or even a supply of old rags to use in scrubbing the hospital. To my astonishment, he picked up two cases of anesthetics!

"What do you call that place?" I asked.

"It's a pharmaceutical supply center," he said. "They are a fine bunch of chaps. They don't always get things in for us when they say they will, but it only means we must anticipate our needs a bit earlier than what might normally be the case."

It was refreshing, to see India through compassionate, understanding eyes. This was their country, and these their people.

"Dr. Sahib! Dr. Sahib!" I heard it again and again as we honked and crept our way through the thronging, narrow streets.

The man in one shop had had cataracts removed only that spring. The child of another had recently been to the hospital for an appendectomy. The attractive housewife, in her bright green sari, had spent a week at Herbertpur recovering from a serious blood infection.

It seemed that everyone in the city knew the doctor and his wife. Knew them and loved them.

As we finally motored out of Dehra Dun, the Lehmanns unwittingly revealed another obvious trait, their pride in the slow but steady progress of India.

"Monica grew up here as a child," Geoffrey said. "Her father served in the army, in the rather famous Jacob's Horse regiment, which I don't suppose you've heard of back in the States. I was here, of course, both of us, some time before Independence." They pointed out a forestry institute, where many different species of trees were being studied. Also a new industrial complex rising above the ancient farmland in declaration of India's unrelenting determination to add the sinews of steel to its national strength.

When we passed through one of the villages, Mrs. Lehmann observed, "It's been a wonderful improvement, the bringing of electricity from the city into little villages like this. People can do so much better for themselves."

As we progressed farther into the country, out into the open places, the scenery came more strikingly into view. To one side a range of jagged, saw-toothed mountains; on the other, the first range of the great Himalayas, with Mussoorie, a good hour's drive away, clearly visible on its grand promontory.

"Are there many churches out here in the country?" I asked.

"There are no churches," the doctor said.

At that moment I thought I saw him take a firmer grip on the wheel.

"It's a pity, really," his wife added. "So many of us have worked so long. We have prayed and prayed."

"Are there no converts?" I asked, remembering my acquaintance with missionaries who had worked exclusively among Tibetans.

The doctor smiled now. "You can find them here and there all over this area," he said. "A terrible price some of them pay to remain true to their faith. They are the church, really. Perhaps only one or two in an occasional village, standing alone as testimony to the grace of God in human hearts."

We all sat quietly now.

A bus loomed out of the dust ahead, holding to the single strip of concrete in the center of the road, as did the doctor, until the last moment before pulling over for a safe meeting. The dust settled on a long caravan of bullock carts, bearing the autumn harvest into Dehra Dun for sale and supplies. Off to my right a team of oxen, yoked to a long pole extended out from a grinding wheel, plodded around and around a worn circle, grinding chappati flour.

And everywhere . . . absolutely everywhere . . . people . . . multitudes of people. This was rural India. These were the common, superstitious, uneducated, hardy, likeable country folk. So greatly in need are these people. In need of education. In need of a better way of life. In need of nourishment the impoverished soil no longer provides.

And in need of someone to show them the way of eternal life and light.

Seated in front of me were two people, Geoffrey and Monica Lehmann, who wanted, more than anything else in their lives, to better the lot of these people and to guide them to knowledge of the Christian faith.

Why were there so few people in the world with this kind of concern? This kind of dedication?

What about my own concern?

My own dedication?

The questions were wind and fire in my heart!

6 When we at last turned off at a small junction onto a road running parallel to a small irrigation canal, I understood why no one ever took a casual trip to Dehra Dun. Yet I could scarcely permit myself to think of journeying weariness with anticipation rising so high in my heart for a first look at the hospital.

It would have one hundred beds, they had told me. I found it difficult to imagine such a structure in an area the like of this. What would be its style of architecture? How would it compare in appearance to the somewhat smaller hospital in my own home town?

Would it exemplify the stewardship philosophy of these people?

I kept wondering.

Then, as I was to subsequently discover, we drove past the hospital without my even seeing. The doctor had turned off the side road onto what had an appearance strikingly similar to a lane leading up to a farmstead set back among its fields. There is a very small village, called Edenbagh as I recall, and just beyond this a cluster of trees. The hospital sat back among these trees, sufficiently camouflaged by the heavy foliage for me to miss it completely.

We came instead to an abrupt turn, and all at once the India of the dusty road had gone. Before us lay a beautiful garden, a kind of arboretum with a large and striking worn brick building in what appeared to be the center of the setting.

"That's the hospital?" I blurted.

It was an awkward question, for the doctor turned and said quietly, "It's our residence."

My eyes fell now in full search across the building, along the fine veranda which reached completely across the length of the imposing front, and for one unpardonable moment my thoughts fell into the frame-of-reference of a coveteous, materialistic American.

I've found him out! I told myself. *A missionary . . . so he is a doctor . . . indulging in this kind of personal luxury!*

The household dogs, Minky and Rufus, heralded our arrival, and a stoic bearer, whose eyes revealed unmistakable love and loyalty for these people, came quickly to unload my luggage and the Lehmanns' bazaar purchases.

A step inside the house, however, brought the first of many moments of self-rebuke. The plain design of the interior was functional and comfortable, the kind of house in which entertainment consists of guests who come and stay and are welcome but must understand that the inhabitants of the house have work to do. I was soon to understand the Lehmanns were like so many others I had met in the harvest hinterlands. People doing many times more than a comparable job demands back home, because so much is required of so few.

"Your house is very nice," I managed to say.

"We lived in a planter's house when we first arrived at Herbertpur," the doctor told me. "The time came when we had to build our own quarters. We knew we were to stay at Herbertpur, for it was so evident the Lord had led us here. We secured this land very cheaply. We cut down our own trees, and made bricks for very little money, and so it was possible to build the hospital and our house here at a mere fraction of what much smaller buildings would cost in England or America."

I took a second look around. The house did have an unmistakable modesty.

"As we thought of the children the Lord would send us," he continued, "we wanted a comfortable, healthy place for them, screened to combat malaria."

The furniture caught my attention now, and further served to incriminate my first impression.

My work takes me to all parts of the United States. Frequently, this involves the privilege of staying in private homes. I have been in wealthy homes, with middle class families, and in America's more humble dwellings, but I could not remember so much as one residence where I had been in the previous ten years where the housewife would have tolerated the antiquity of the furniture in the house at Herbertpur. Yet that furniture was part of the charm of the place. Sturdily built, in the style of the American parlor just before the advent of overstuffed sofas and chairs, it had surely been brought in with the first opening of the house, a few pieces no doubt having been used in the temporary place of residence the Lehmanns secured when they first came out from England.

I have come to think of that house as one of the most charming and interesting I have ever known. I really can't say why. I think it is because the house has feel to it, as well as sight. It has a personality which can no more be defined than can the personal magnetism of a complete stranger.

One long corridor reaches nearly the length of the entire structure, with a much shorter intercepting corridor at the farthest end.

The door to my room was at the center of this short corridor.

It was a rather large room, high-ceilinged like the rest of the house for maximum comfort in hot weather. The two beds were of the plainest wood design, giving the appearance of having been fashioned by makeshift carpentry. In keeping with the rest of the house, the room had a characteristic neatness, the deft touch of the homemaker much too occupied with other things to be concerned about lavishness, yet somehow finding the time to add the touch of her graciousness to provisions made for house guests.

I could not resist the compulsion to drop to my knees for a moment, thanking God for the awesome immensity of His goodness in bringing me to Herbertpur. I told Him I knew He meant this experience to be meaningful beyond the blueprinting of a motion picture. Herbertpur was a hidden place, far removed from television antennas and two car garages and rigamarole functions and the million other things that have sometimes left my heart weary. Here was a spiritual freshness, a calculated dynamic, a God-ruled mood.

I wanted my heart to be open to all that I might learn from my stay here.

7 A visitor to Herbertpur soon learns what is perhaps the most characteristic trait of the Lehmanns. At the train station, they were relaxed and casual, as though they had met me for a joint holiday. This attitude prevailed during the shopping tour around Dehra Dun, and across the twenty-five dusty miles to their home.

Moments after we entered the house, however, Dr. Lehmann looked at his watch and said, "We have done quite well. I've just enough time to get ready for my morning rounds."

His wife said, "I'll get right over to the dispensary. They'll be needing several of the things we picked up in town."

At that moment, the casualness was gone. It would not be correct to say they became tense. In fact, one of the enviable capacities of these two people is the ability to face complex responsibilities with outright candor. The simple reason is that both the hours of the day and the responsibilities of their work have been fitted into such well organized patterns that, so long as the routines are not disturbed, each day moves with remarkable smoothness.

But when the time comes for a given responsibility, and during the time alloted for that responsibility, the dynamic dedication of these people becomes fully observable.

The doctor walks with brisk steps. He has one or two characteristic expressions, which I observed to be a kind of audible signal, like the horn on the Land Rover, warning idlers to clear the path. It is not that he becomes thoughtless of others. Quite the contrary. But it does mean the time has come for him to give full concentration to duty.

Even so, he came and tapped on my door, and asked if I would like to go with him on his morning rounds since, at the meeting in England, we had discussed the possibility of including the hospital in a sequence or two of the forthcoming film.

We followed a cement block walk leading away from the house. I noticed that the blocks were precisely spaced to accomodate the doctor's brisk step. Very little consequence now, but doubtless indispensible during the wet weeks of the monsoon.

In a moment, we stepped through a small gate. Behind us lay the house and the restful gardens. Beyond, once more, lay India. The hospital courtyard, thronged with people, like the streets of Dehra Dun, like the villages we had passed through. At first glimpse of the doctor, a dozen or more clamored for his attention.

Like plaintive children, they pointed to the ailing areas of their bodies, their eyes solemn in the assurance that *Daktar Limon Sahib* could prescribe just the magic potion needed to assuage their ills.

When the doctor told the patients they needed to wait until the appointed hour for examinations, one old fellow turned to me, thinking if he couldn't get the head doctor to listen to his tale of woe, he might do well to settle for a lesser medic. There was a time in my life when I had thought of becoming a doctor, so this became a brief moment of vicarious delight.

"You designed the hospital?" I asked, as the doctor hurried on.

A brief glance about the compound had shown me this was not only a large plant, but one which had been carefully planned.

"Designed it and supervised every square inch of construction," the doctor answered. "I was an engineer, you know, fully trained for engineering, that is."

"If you told me, I didn't remember," I said, suspecting another facet of this man's colorful life which might one day be worth the telling.

We came now to the main entrance of the hospital. Here stood a younger doctor, gently telling a patient he must wait his turn to be seen. The patient left, and the man turned to us. He was tall and fine featured and a smile came full and warm upon his face.

He was Dr. Peter Warlow, whom I would watch again and again performing intricate surgical feats, and with whom I would go often from ward to ward, as he looked after the physical needs of his patients. For the moment, however, our initial meeting was brief.

33

A male nurse appeared, carrying a tray of dressings, and Dr. Lehmann and the nurse and I entered the male ward. The doctor, sensing my somewhat startled reaction, took a moment to say, "Quite different from what one is accustomed to back home, isn't it? We have found that the more we allow patients to live as they are accustomed to living in their homes, the more quickly they respond to treatment. We insist on cleanliness in surgery and in dressings and when giving injections, but the more general aspects of hospital life, as you can well see, might seem to leave a great deal to be desired."

"*Ap kaise hain?*" the doctor asked, inquiring about the progress of an old man.

"*Ap mujhe thik kar sakte hain,*" the old fellow replied. I was told he expressed full confidence in the doctor's ability to restore him to good health.

The doctor checked his chart and his pulse, and gave the nurse instructions for continued treatment.

"*Afsos, afsos,*" the patient moaned as we moved on.

"We scrub the floors every morning," the doctor continued, "but it doesn't help much when patients won't cooperate. It may not look like it now, but the ward is also swept clean once a day. The only trouble is, many of these patients have the inborn idea that the main purpose of the broom is to sweep up whatever debris they may have a notion to throw onto the floor."

I thought back to magazine articles I had read, criticising the hospital established by Dr. Albert Schweitzer at Lambarene. Again and again, during the days at Herbertpur, I found myself comparing the two doctors. There is a good deal of similarity between them. Both were fully educated in one field, decided instead to study medicine. Both had strong humanitarian compulsions.

Schweitzer's approach to hospital sanitation, as I understand it, is complicated by his almost fanatic esteem for all forms of life. Dr. Lehmann, who has given thought to the Schweitzer approach in medical missions, likes to tell the story of the visitor who came to Lambarene and walked with Schweitzer one day along a jungle trail.

A large beetle appeared on the path, and the visitor stepped forward to trample it.

Schweitzer, however, restrained him. Pointing to the frightened beetle, as it disappeared into the green oblivion, Schweitzer said, "Remember, my friend, you and I are visitors in his country."

That first experience of ward rounds brought to my attention a noteworthy and refreshing difference between the doctor from Herbertpur and a host of other medical missionaries. It became soon evident from his bedside and consultation manner. To every one, a kind word, and whenever possible, a gentle reminder that faith in *Yesu Masih* is far more important than health of body.

I said, "The way you combine witness with your work is very refreshing."

He finished giving instructions to the male nurse, paused a moment, looked up and smiled.

"The philosophy of some medical missionaries is to give full attention to the medical work, which draws patients to the hospital, and then delegate evangelists and Bible women to take responsibility for spiritual contacts. That is a sad mistake."

"The argument I've heard," I said, "is that the medical missionary has so much to do he cannot possibly serve beyond his medical responsibilites."

"Nothing is more important than personal witness. A Christian who does not witness, in my opinion, is a Christian who is not fulfilling God's purpose in his life."

"I take it you have a definite philosophy along this line here at Herbertpur."

"We certainly do," he replied, "In fact, we put it this way. We are not medical missionaries; we are missionary medics. That's quite a difference."

We moved on now down to the female ward, where an attractive young lady, an Indian nurse, joined us.

"Should I wait outside?" I asked.

"Come on in," the doctor said, "It's quite all right."

Not medical missionaries, but missionary medics. The words lingered long in my thoughts, and I transposed their meaning to a multitude of other situations. To people busy in church functions, serving on committees, occupying a pew whenever the church door opens, around and around and around and in and out, wearing a beaten path between their home and the church.

And yet never once, not even to their own children, rising to the prime function for which every child of God is responsible.

I thought of the final words of Jesus, the last thing He said on earth before ascending into heaven, *"Ye shall be witnesses unto me."*

Missionary medics . . .

God helping me, the meaning of those words must never relax my own spiritual consciousness.

From the female ward, we moved over just a few steps to the eye wards.

Here the good doctor stood to his full height, for this is the heart of his medical interest and skill.

So far removed from the commotions of the western world and far too busy to concern himself with writing for medical journals, it is quite likely the name Dr. Geoffrey D. Lehmann has never been officially associated with the great names in the world of ophthalmology. But I feel constrained to think it could be. During the days that followed, as I sat tense and hushed, watching the doctor at work in the eye theatre, it may have been mounting prejudice in his favor, but I had a strong suspicion few surgeons anywhere in the world could have exceeded his prowess.

He took a moment to show me the eye theatre, a windowless room designed by the doctor for best methodology.

"I'm very proud of this," he said, lifting a wooden box. "It's our Beta Ray Therapy unit." He lifted the top, and brought out a pencil-like projection. "You've perhaps heard of Strontium 90, a product of the atomic age. We use this in certain cases of eye damage, to prevent the formation of scar tissue. We've had really marvelous results with it."

He told me of a young man, blinded by an explosion, who heard of Herbertpur and traveled nearly a thousand miles to come for treatment. He had gone to Bombay and Calcutta, seeking help, but was sent home to face the remainder of his life groping.

Two hundred miles from Herbertpur, the guide who had offered to help him reach his destination grew weary of the trek and abandoned him. By sheer pluck, he came alone the rest of the way.

"My heart sank as I examined his eyes," the doctor told me. "He could see light, but nothing more. We decided to operate."

The doctor opened minute windows in both eyes, in an effort to restore vision. The difficulty in such a case is that, after a few weeks, the cleared area scars over again and vision is lost.

"But with the application of Beta Ray Therapy, a unit I purchased in the United States, by the way, we were able to prevent the growth of blood vessels and keep the cornea transparent. After a few weeks, he was able to walk about. He went home by himself. But before he left, he told us not only was he going home with his vision restored, but he was going home with the new life Christ gives in his heart, determined to tell others what the Lord Jesus meant to him."

Not medical missionaries.

Missionary medics!

Where can one observe a scene more moving than that of a man or a woman from one of India's destitute villages, as the doctor tenderly removes the bandages from their eyes and, in so doing, reintroduces them to those dimensions of life which can only be experienced by physical sight?

"What do these people pay for a cataract operation?" I asked.

He smiled. "Five rupees, ten perhaps . . . fifteen if we are sure they can afford so much. It is good for a man to pay something. Of course, when we believe a case is destitute, we charge nothing."

Five rupees! On foreign exchange charts, that's just a few pennies more than an American one dollar bill.

For five rupees, one of earth's lowly people could benefit from surgery which, back in New York or Chicago or your home town, would cost a thousand dollars and more.

"Do these people realize how much they are receiving for so little?" I asked. "Talking with a student coming up on the train, I was told a man can earn three or four rupees a day working on a road building job."

"That's true," the doctor said, "and there are farmers, especially when crops are poor, who will go away for periods of time to obtain such employment. However, these people tend to think of as little as five rupees as a lot of money."

"Surely, though," I interrupted, "they must understand that a surgeon spends a great deal of time and money preparing himself."

"Perhaps some of them realize," the doctor said, "Whenever possible we get them to pay the basic costs for the medicines we dispence. Even for this, we maintain a charity fund. I would say most of the people who come to the hospital are appreciative of what the Lord enables us to do for them. However, I doubt if very many of them comprehend economic aspects."

"I take it you aren't particularly interested in having them feel as though they are receiving charity."

"These are human beings. Just because they are eminently less fortunate than we are doesn't mean they have no personal dignity. They do have dignity. We do our best to respect it."

"How do you determine the amount of payment in any given case?"

"It is not always easy to decide. At one time we had different colored papers on which names were printed and prescriptions written. Each color indicated what was estimated to be each patient's economic bracket. But they quickly caught on to this. Now we have a special sign, which looks much the same as medical terminology."

"Do some patients try to cheat the hospital?"

"I suppose you'd call it that. They will complain about how difficult they have it in life, hoping for free treatment. They will dress in their poorest, like one patient who about had me agreed to treat him at our lowest figure when my wife came in to ask who had arrived in the big American car parked just outside the compound. It turned out this fellow had come in the car.

"But many of the dear people who come are really poverty stricken, with scarcely enough money to feed themselves, and we try to give them every consideration.

"One thing we must be careful of is not to give the impression our medical work is meant to buy people's favor. A Tibetan lama spent several days at the hospital, and was quite put out when I told him he must pay. 'You will gain much spiritual merit from treating me, a lama,' he said. 'You should pay me for coming to the hospital!' Needless to say, we found his argument quite unconvincing."

We moved now to another eye ward, where

the doctor spent several minutes examining patients. He would not, however, forget the subject of our discussion.

As soon as he was occupied once more with details which did not require concentration or interrogation of a patient, he said, "It is the farthest thing from our purpose to win the confidence of anyone in India by economic persuasion. The Indian government declares itself to be completely secular, and looks with strongest disfavor at proselytizing."

"Proselytizing?" I asked. " You mean they are opposed to conversion?"

"By proselytizing," he explained, "we mean winning people to a Christian commitment through economic benefits. It has happened far too often. We take great care in preventing its happening here. Our desire is to perform the best possible medical service we can. Then, when people come to our hospital, we seek to show them, through our lives, that Christ has set us free from spiritual bondage, just as He can set them free."

He moved once again to another patient, and once again gave a reassuring pat on the arm with a warm word in the Hindustani tongue.

As I stood watching, I could not resist a silent prayer. The compulsion continued throughout those many days at the hospital. Whenever I was with the doctors and staff members, I prayed that God would help them to find, with each patient, that moment of opportunity when they might speak of the love of God and the saving power in the death and resurrection of *Yesu Masih.*

From the eye wards, we crossed once again through the main courtyard, alongside the wall and a small tea shop operated as a private concession for the convenience of patients. Again, the doctor was accosted by sufferers who found comfort in the momentary glance he gave a large goiter or an ulcerated arm or a pair of eyes gone blind.

A nurse came by, pausing only momentarily for a word of greeting. She was Annette Warlow, wife of the other doctor.

"She and Peter are a wonderful addition to our work," Dr. Lehmann told me, as we moved on. "We are always so short of staff, and everyone must perform several duties. Mrs. Warlow helps in so many phases of the work, but her general responsibility is to serve as staff matron. One must always take great care to maintain good relations with national help, especially when the pressure of work is as heavy as it is here, and Mrs. Warlow is very kind and gentle and tactful with our Indian co-workers. It helps immensely."

We came to the private rooms, a motel-like line of individual compartments, for use by those who wished to pay for this kind of accommodation as well as those so critically ill they needed added quiet and special attention.

A missionary nurse was on duty, and after having grown accustomed to British accents on the part of other Westerners I had met thus far, it took only a phrase from her lips to inform me she was an American.

The only American on the staff, I learned, a Miss Esther Kuhns from Seattle.

She had been on duty throughout the night, and would normally have gone to her bungalow to rest long before now, but a woman from the Jaunsari tribe high in the hills had come in, critically ill with fever, and so she had remained on duty.

"You must get some rest, Esther," the doctor said.

"I will," she told him, "just as soon as I can."

"So many of our patients in other phases of the work are with us for such a short time," the doctor said, as we moved on. "This, of course, is good for their sakes, but since our greatest concern is always to confront these people with the Gospel message, the more time we have with them, the better."

We arrived now at the TB block, a compact little building with entrances only from the outside through separate doorways to each room. The rooms were small, with wide, screened openings on all sides just below the roof to admit a maximum amount of fresh air without denying privacy to the patient.

"We have worked out a rather good arrangement with the TB patients," the doctor continued. "Tubercularies continue six months to a year, and so we divide the time into two periods. The length, of course, depends upon each patient's individual need. We charge a nominal fee for the patient during the first period, while he is in the block, and then we tell him that during the entire duration of the second period, at which time he lives at home but comes in for frequent examination, all medicines and examinations are free-of-charge. It works like a charm. TB is the white plague to these people, and they fear it desperately. So there is seldom any problem to keep them for the first part of treatment. Then, afterwards, knowing they are receiving the medicines and examinations free, they come back regularly in accordance with our plan."

We talked more as the doctor went from room to room examining patients. Several came from the sweeper class, the lowest of India's castes, but there were also farmers, merchants, and the doctor told me members of the highest caste, the Brahmins, sometimes come for treatment.

At this particular time, the doctor's favorite patient was a lovely girl from the Jaunsari tribe. The Jaunsaris, who are Hindu in their religion, stem from Arayan rather than Oriental ethnic background, with fair skin and features and hair like the women of Europe and North America.

"There is a scarcity of women among the Jaunsaris," the doctor told me. "As a consequence, they practice polyandry. A woman may have as many as four husbands, usually all brothers, and since women are so scarce, the wife usually receives good treatment. We must arrange for you to visit a Jaunsari village up in the hills. Unfortunately I can't take you back as far as I would like due to the military situation between India and Red China, but there are a few Jaunsaris living out in more accessible areas."

His eyes brightened a moment. "Perhaps you could introduce some of their colorful customs in a sequence of the film."

Now he grew serious once more.

He had shown me progress charts on several occasions. It was remarkable, almost startling in some cases, the quick response to treatment. Little wonder, with the white plague so universally feared among these people and with modern medicine so effective, the TB block was always full.

"We have some of our most effective spiritual results among the TB patients," he said. "It is because they are with us for a longer time, and can become more familiar with Christian teaching. In other areas of the hospital, our patients often do not recognize the seriousness of their situation. They sometimes steal away in the night to return to their homes."

"Do those who are seriously ill ever leave in this way?" I asked.

"Yes. Some years ago, before Peter came, I had attempted plastic surgery on a woman's nose. This required a temporary connection of her nose with her arm. We realized she was becoming a bit impatient, but never dreamed she would walk away one night, her nose grown securely to her arm."

"Did she ever return?" I asked.

"We never saw her again."

"She spent the rest of her life with her nose connected to her arm?"

"It's possible. More likely, though, she found some enterprising quack who did the separation for her. She would certainly spend the remainder of her life with a badly-marred face."

When he had finished with the last patient in the block, and stood talking with me for a moment, the sound of singing came from the direction of the hospital courtyard.

"Let's get back quickly," he said, promptly setting a fast pace down the walk. "Mr. Mall, our Indian evangelist, has begun the Gospel service, and it means so much to the patients if they see those of us on the staff participating."

Again the doctor's words echoed in my thoughts. *Not medical missionaries, but missionary medics!*

8 When an Englishman speaks of having a "spot of tea," he converses in the spirit of Empire, but the British did not adapt this hearty host to their health until their ships went sailing down along the Spanish Main and across the length of Africa and around the Cape of Good Hope, on and on seaward beyond India to the farthest surf of Oriental waters.

Chinese legend has it that Emperor Shen-nung first discovered the benefits of the bracing beverage in 277 B.C. and the Chinese trace all medicinal and agricultural knowledge of the leaf back to that day. They tell the story of a Bodhidharma, an ascetic Buddhist from India, who came on a preaching trek into China. While there, he vowed to sit in contemplation of Buddha's virtues nine years without sleep.

When three years had passed, however, he dropped off into slumber and, angry at himself, cut off his eyelids and threw them to the ground beside him.

Five more years passed and again drowsiness plagued his meditation. Noticing some leaves on a shrub nearby, he pulled them off and chewed on them, finding stimulation to fulfill his nine years vow, thus elevating the tea leaf to a place in the sun.

In any case, it is said to be an Englishman representing the East India Company who wrote a letter from Japan in June of 1615, to another officer of the company in Macao, mentioning "a pot of the best sort of chaw."

By the middle of the 17th century, the English were well along in the development of their taste for tea, and in an old British magazine, dated December 1658, one finds the following advertising copy:

> *That excellent and by all physi-tians approved China Drink called by the Chineans Tcha, by other nations Tay, alias Tee, is sold at the Sultaness Head, a copheehouse in Sweetings Runts, by the Royal Exchange, London.*

And a British writer of the same era, describing the drink, writes, "In respect of its scarceness and dearness, it hath been only used in a regalia in high treatments and entertainments, and presents made thereof to princes and grandees."

All of which is meant to emphasize that, wherever the British flag has flown, tea is the national drink. The hospital at Herbertpur, in fact, sits in a veritable nest of tea plantations, most of which still have British connections, and Heinz Fussle and I had a most interesting discussion one morning with a young tea planter who has ever since kept our household supplied with the finest of his crop.

And so it was to be expected in the Lehmann home that, morning and afternoon at the proper time, tea was served. Sometimes in the parlor, sometimes on the back veranda, sometimes under the huge, wide-spreading pipal tree which stood very near the house.

Personally, I have never been able to muster any substantial enthusiasm for tea, although I don't mind drinking it, and I presumed at first that one of the shortest routes to the Doctor's heart would be by way of the cup. There is a certain charm to the English tea time. Mrs. Lehmann, as dedicated and industrious a woman as I've ever met, took special pains on her trips to Dehra Dun to select pastries which would add a tasteful touch to tea time.

I must confess, though, that whenever the occasion would allow, not only in the Lehmann home but in similar commonwealth situations, I often sought excuse to be unavailable at the hour of tea.

Imagine my surprise, as well as my amusement, when the good doctor caught me in the act of missing tea one day and most happily became a partner in my folly, confessing that he, too, sometimes chaffed at the frequency of serving.

Through all of this, however, let me say that tea time can be most engaging, and some of our finest conversations occurred during these hours. There were even occasions when I succumbed to a second cup.

I especially remember one of our earliest liquid repasts, as we sat on the back veranda.

I had wanted to talk with the doctor about personal stewardship ever since Alan Norrish, for whom we now had a crew at work producing *India Today*, told me about the unique dedication which had made Herbertpur Hospital possible.

So, being as candidly frank as I could, I broached the subject.

"It's a matter we rarely discuss," the doctor said.

"You are to be commended," I told him. "Christians in America, who do far less, often go to some length to make sure their alms do not go unnoticed."

He sipped his tea quietly, as I waited for him to say more.

When he didn't, I continued. I told him the work at the hospital had a strong grip on my heart. A certain amount of fascination could be expected, of course, for work so unique and so far away, but it was more than this. There seemed to be a special formula functioning here, human dedication aligned with divine blessing in the most unusual procedure.

"The world needs to know about this," I said.

It was plain to see from the look on his face that he was dubious of my suggestion.

"Really, Doctor," I pressed further, "from a human point of view, I believe the story of your work would interest thousands of people all over the world. But I'm thinking beyond the human element."

He broke in saying, "But ours is only one of many missionary hospitals."

"At first look, yes. I've been taking a second look. I do not know of another hospital such as this anywhere in the world."

He put down his tea cup, leaned forward slightly. I took encouragement.

"I can understand your natural hesitancy about this, coming from a stranger such as myself, but I'm becoming more and more convinced that what has happened . . . first in your heart and then here at Herbertpur . . . needs to be made known to thinking Christians all over the world."

"We are quite eager for the ministry of Herbertpur to be made known," he said, "but I'm not sure either Monica or I could agree to anything beyond that."

"Have you considered your responsibility in the matter?"

"My responsibility?"

I nodded. "A great battle is on in the Christian church today. To me, it's nothing less than Satanic. I'm not sufficiently familiar with Christians in England to voice an opinion, but I think I understand the situation in America quite well, if for no other reason than the conflicts which have been engaged in my own heart."

I saw something begin to happen in his eyes. I had seen it before in my relationships with the English.

It would perhaps be unkind to say the British distrust Americans. Instead, and surely not without good reason, the Englishman tends to think of an American as his younger brother. He loves that brother, and because he loves him, he puts up with what he considers his many immaturities, but he does not quickly take the younger brother's counsel or instruction.

But there are exceptions, of course, when an Englishman concedes that the younger brother has at least come to sufficient years for his words to deserve a hearing.

I felt this moment had come in my relationship with this great man. Not that he recognized in me any tall example of wisdom but, rather, his willingness to participate in the spiritual concern of any fellow Christian who recognized within the church stimuli giving rise to indifference and outright lethargy.

With the passing of time, I was to understand another aspect of this man which prompted his sense of fraternity with Americans. Long before, at least inwardly, he had revolted against the demands of convention. First and foremost, people are people, the doctor believes. I would hesitate to put the words into his mouth, but I often got the idea he would have thought our world a happier place if a few British would be a bit more like Americans and, to be sure, if a few Americans would be a bit more like the English.

In any case, he expressed willingness to hear what I had to say.

"The American Christian," I began, "is caught in the grip of materialism. Nearly everyone lives just a shade above his income. As his income rises, so does his standard of living. Whether or not the average Christian tithes, I can't say, and that's not the issue, really. The issue is that the average American Christian equates God's blessing on his life, not in spiritual terms but in economic terms."

"I'm afraid you'll find this true in England and on the European continent as well," the doctor said.

"I've been here long enough to discover how pitifully shorthanded you are in the hospital. I'd like for you to tell me more about this. But yours is not an isolated situation. Take, for example, those five wonderful young men who gave their lives on Palm Beach, in an effort to make contact with the pagan Aucas of Ecuador's Oriente jungle. One of the mission boards involved . . . one of the fellows at Palm Beach was on assignment with them . . . recently issued a statement that, for the first time in the mission's history, they did not have one candidate.

"As I understand it, this is a small mission. However, I heard recently that one of the largest independent mission boards in America

51

issued an urgent prayer call to its closest constituents. Although this mission board has sent hundreds of missionaries to the field, the time came, the first time in their history, when they were not processing so much as one candidate."

"It's frightening, isn't it?" the doctor observed. "To what do you attribute this?"

"I'm not sure," I replied, "but there seems to be a kind of rebellious spiritual spirit in the world. It's as though we Christians are all swept up in a tidal onrush. So, in a sense, the Christian cannot help himself. That is, he is not to blame for the fact that this wrong spirit exists.

"But the problem, as I see it, is the reluctance of those American leaders who influence Christian thought, and who ought to be leading the way back to proper spiritual values. Instead of recognizing the problem, and doing something about it, these people, in my opinion, seem to be contributing to the difficulty."

"In what way?"

"Well, take the church itself. By this, I don't mean the Body of Christ as such, but the organized church, the individual congregation. I'm sure it has happened without many sincere Christians realizing it, but materialistic concepts have begun to actually take over the church."

"For example?"

"The tendency of many congregations is to think quantitatively rather than qualitatively. Success lies in numbers and economic strength, rather than in productive victory within the individual Christian's heart and life.

"In a great number of the Christian schools with which America is abundantly blessed, the emphasis tends to be away from Christian service. It sounds good, challenging students to become professional and civic leaders, and I'm sure there is spiritual value to this in proper balance. Yet people I have often observed quite obviously do not first think of becoming prosperous doctors, lawyers, businessmen and the like in order to be good stewards but, rather, that they may first of all have a comfortable way of life."

I told him of my own Alma Mater. During my time on campus, students preparing for Christian service composed by far the largest single group. Today, a mere fraction of the student body is preparing for what we have come to call full-time Christian service.

Parents are making a kind of cult out of their children. They want them to succeed. They want them to gain prominence. Education is not for the purpose of studying *to show thyself approved unto God* but, rather, to insure a good paycheck.

"Today's Christian must face up to the fact that no one can serve two masters." I said, "We cannot serve God and Mammon."

He sat quietly, waiting for me to continue, and I breathed a prayer of thanks and a request for guidance.

"The telling of your story could bring conviction and provide guidance for many Christians who need to be brought face on with the fact that stewardship involves more than token remembrance of God. It would be one of the finest opportunities of my life, if you were to give me permission to make this story known."

"Well," he mused, clasping his hands and studying them for a moment, "you have me backed into a corner."

"I've written quite a number of magazine articles, personality stories about Christians and their activities," I went on, "and I have often encountered those who, in all sincerity, hesitate to have their stories published. So let me put it this way. Suppose you had an opportunity to sit down here, as we are doing now, and give the witness of your life, what God has done for you and through you, to, let's say, a hundred thousand Christians."

"I suppose I would leap at the opportunity."

"The feat can be accomplished quite easily, simply by putting your story into print."

Now he grew hesitant again.

And so I opened my own heart a bit more. I told him how, as a young Christian, I found myself drawn more and more into the net of relating God's blessing to His provision of physical need. My childhood and early youth spanned the Great Depression, giving me a stirring restlessness to rise above economic depravity. So, as a young writer, I found myself attracted increasingly to dollar signs. The more money I had in the bank, the more sure I was that God was on my side.

Then in 1948, Bob Pierce, founder of the World Vision organization, invited me to travel with him on his second trip to the Orient, assisting in the production of a motion picture and writing magazine features plus a book on missions in China. It was my first look at the world's other side, and it tore my heart free from the materialistic shackles which had begun to so firmly enslave me.

"Maybe I think out of balance, Dr. Lehmann," I said. "Help me on this if you can. But, somehow, I feel it takes an affinity to missions for a Christian to see God's total purposes in clear focus."

"Missionary work has certainly been God's way of bringing fulfillment into my own life," the doctor said.

"That's just it! That word, fulfillment. As I understand it, you and your wife both come from prominent backgrounds. You could have chosen any place on earth to live. You could have provided for yourselves the material-istic way of life in which so many American Christians indulge. But you didn't. I think the world needs to know this. It's not a matter of your story so much . . . you as a given indi-vidual . . . but rather the principles involved. The principles of stewardship, obedience, dedication."

Once again he remained quietly thoughtful for a moment.

"I suppose I should say let's have a go at it," he said at last. "Monica and I surely do want whatever the Lord wants. You'll be here for several more days. Let me have some time to think about it. I want to talk to Monica. We both need some time to pray."

He poured us each another cup of tea.

9 Immediately after breakfast each week-day morning, the hospital staff meets to worship in a little chapel. It stands alone in a cluster of trees, just off the walk between the worker's quarters and the hospital, and a small bell somewhat discordantly, but joy-fully, announces the time for gathering.

Usually the punctual doctor rings it himself.

In true English fashion, a cemetery lies alongside the chapel, modest footstones marking the graves of staff members and Indian Christians laid to rest. One headstone, identical in shape to the others, designates the grave of Dr. Lehmann's mother, who passed away while on a visit from England.

The half hour worship is called "Prayers," which is also typically British, and consists of several songs, a Bible message and a time of intercession. There are no pews. Everyone sits on the floor.

The Lehmanns are Plymouth Brethren, so the women sit apart and quiet during worship, but they participate with enthusiasm in the singing. The songs are all in Hindustani, but after a few mornings, the visitor begins to recognize some of the phrases.

Many of the tunes are national in origin, but some of the great western hymns have also been translated. I particularly remember *Crown Him Lord of All*, with its magnificent phrase, *"Tum jano Shahansha."* Christ, instead of being depicted as the Lord of Lords, is more accurately portrayed to the Indian mind as the Shah who is above all shahs!

Quite often, Dr. Peter Warlow is in charge, and he gives a touch of compelling sincerity and radiance to the conduct of the meeting.

I especially enjoyed the preaching of Mr. Mall, the hospital evangelist. He always spoke in Hindustani, putting me at considerable disadvantage, but the unction of his soul spread across his face like the glow of the morning. On occasion, he likes to drop in an English phrase, possibly the words of a song or a verse of Scripture.

His favorite quotation, which I only heard once but was told he uses over and over, consists of the immortal words from Longfellow's *A Psalm of Life.*

> *Lives of great men all remind us*
> *We can make our lives sublime*
> *And, departing, leave behind us*
> *Footprints on the sands of time.*

One of the first mornings, when prayers had concluded, and, in accordance with Indian custom we walked barefoot to the entrance doorway to put on our shoes, Dr. Warlow said to me, "I'll be in surgery for most of the morning, beginning in about twenty minutes. Would you like to have a look?"

"You're sure you don't mind?"

"Not at all. You are quite welcome."

I hurried over to the main theatre, put on sterile clothes, face mask and bonnet, and stepped into the operating room just as two male nurses brought the first patient.

Step by step, as though I were a medical student, Dr. Warlow took me through each stage of the procedure. It was a memorable experience to watch him at work.

In all cases that morning, his diagnosis had been correct. The knife became a wand of mercy, relieving pain and prolonging life.

I could not help comparing Dr. Warlow with the typical medic back in America. I have no desire to censure these men, but I have met many an MD whom I would have liked to have seen spend a morning with Peter Warlow, witnessing his skill and his dedication and, to me most important of all, his human and spiritual warmth. There was none of the vaunted, impersonal air so often characteristic in American physicians and surgeons.

The sun had risen to high noon by the time he finished.

"I'd like to go with you on ward rounds sometime, if I may," I told him. I was anxious to see this phase of his conduct as well.

"Whenever you wish," he said. "I'll be going this afternoon. Should I stop by for you?"

So it was agreed.

I had a half hour in my room before the great corridor gong was sounded, announcing the meal.

I remember walking to the window to stand and look out at the great eucalyptus and at the garden. There was such a unique personality to everything. Even the garden, a result of many seasons of planning and planting, symbolized the purposes of these magnificent people. They were a garden, an oasis of hope and meaning to the people of this great northern area.

The truth of that analogy was to be revealed with increasing clarity that afternoon, as Dr. Warlow took me on ward rounds.

A Nepalese man, badly maimed in an explosion, lay in much pain. The doctor spoke to him in quiet, assuring tones, but the fear did not leave the man's face.

Perhaps he would not remain at the hospital long enough to gain any real comprehension of the reality of human kindness. His view of life and the world consisted of the kind of conduct that caused his employer to leave him abandoned along the roadside following his injury.

On another bed lay an old Tibetan man, his diagnosis not yet complete. Dr. Warlow said he would probably need surgery, but only after every attempt had been made to build strength into his racked, weary frame.

There is a world on every man's face, the worn marks of his world, and nowhere does one realize this with more impact than on the mission field.

As I stood at the Tibetan man's cotside, I said, "What would you give, Peter, to break through that man's shell and be able to really show Christ to him?"

The young doctor shook his head. "It is one of our greatest discouragements," he said. "A tremendous challenge, never to settle for defeat. We do all we can. We try to show love and kindness to them. We give them the best of care. Then we pray that the Holy Spirit will use these efforts as a window, you might say, perhaps not to reveal Christ to them, since they have so far to come before they can begin to have any real kind of spiritual insight, but to at least put a hunger in their hearts. If their spiritual curiosity can be aroused, if they become aware of their heart-hunger, then they begin to listen."

"I suppose at first they scarcely know what they're listening to."

"That's right."

"It's too bad more people don't understand this," I said. "So many Americans have the idea all a missionary has to do is appear in a given place, give a Gospel message, and converts are won as a matter of course."

Dr. Warlow shook his head slowly, and we moved out of the male ward and into the female ward.

A couple of women, instructed to remain bedfast, had ventured partway across the large room. At the appearance of the doctor, they scampered back to their beds like little children, giggling with delight at the excitement of being caught.

They had a good excuse for their mischief, however.

Emmy, the only name by which I ever heard her called, was with them. Emmy is a retired missionary, living out her retirement on the mission field! Together with Mrs. Mall, Emmy was using old Christmas cards and Sunday school pictures, sent second-hand from abroad, to illustrate a Bible story.

"She's won many people to Christ, in her loving and gentle way," Dr. Warlow said.

Our next stop took us to a private room, which I was surprised to find crowded with people.

"*Salaam,*" the young doctor greeted.

"*Salaamji!*" came a chorus response.

In India, as in many other similar areas, family members accompany the patient to the hospital. There is no such thing, for example, as a hospital kitchen. Each family provides for its own.

As we elbowed our way into the room, dimly lit because the shades were full drawn, I saw a woman, lying on a lone bed, her face taut with pain.

"These are relatives?" I asked.

Dr. Warlow nodded, said, "Her case is quite pitiful. She was struck by lightning and badly burned on one entire side of her body."

"How did it happen?"

"We had such a job looking after her when they brought her in yesterday, I didn't have a chance to find out any of the details. I'll see what I can learn now."

He went to the bedside, spoke again with the gentle warmth which is so much a trademark of the Herbertpur hospital.

"The burn extends from here," he said, pointing to her shoulder, "all the way to her foot."

He then gave some instructions to the nurse, after which he turned and addressed the men in the room.

"*Ap men se kaun is ka shauhar hai?*" he asked. Turning to me, he explained, "I've asked which is her husband."

The situation was much too serious for me to be amused when three of the men responded that each of them was one of her husbands.

"*Us ko kaise chot lagi?*" the doctor asked.

One of the husbands, apparently the spokesman, replied "*Daktar Sahib, bahut bari bijli se chot lagi.*"

"He says she was struck by a very big lightning," the doctor interpreted.

The man chattered on for a few moments, and though I could not understand his words, the anguished hurt in his voice was as universal as the sight of tears.

Bit by bit, the Doctor ferreted out the story.

They were hill people, their home built of hewn and gathered rocks, mortared and fitted in the sturdy but simple structure so typical in the highlands.

They feared the storms.

Pity welled up in my heart, as Dr. Warlow pieced together the story from the bits of information they gave him.

It was plain to see how strong a part superstition played in their lives. The angry skies. The harsh voice of the thunder. Gigantic, sword-like thrusts of the lightning. Somehow, the gods had looked with displeasure upon the inhabitants of their home. Perhaps one of them had unwittingly desecrated a tree or a bush or a spot of ground sacred to the spirits or, even more likely, one of them in a previous life, before his present reincarnation, had conducted himself in such a way that the gods, always quick to revenge, chose to strike through the bolt of lightning.

In any case, the sky-borne bolt had wrapped itself around the dwelling, like a serpent of fire, and had found one tiny crack in the mortar. The chief husband measured with his thumb and his forefinger to emphasize the smallness of the fissure. Through this minute opening, the lightning had leaped into the room, striking dead two adults and a small child in the arms of the woman who lay suffering before us.

It has long disturbed me that people, who identify quickly with physical need and suffering, face unmoved an example of spiritual need. The church at home gives liberally, when confronted with the need for physical mercy, but too often fails to meet its responsibility and its opportunity in instances of spiritual plight.

Be that as it may, a heart of stone could not have looked at that woman and felt no pity. But as we lingered there in the room, the deepest cry that came to my heart was for the spiritual need of these people.

A bolt of lightning. Tragic consequence. To be sure. But far more cataclysmic was the fact that these poor souls were, at that moment, devoid of the capacity to look to God for help.

God . . . *Bhagwan* they called Him . . . in whatever moment they might have occasion to think of one deity as being supreme above any others. But they had never heard such words as *The Lord is my Shepherd . . . Know ye that the Lord, He is God . . . I will never leave thee nor forsake thee.*

"It's a terrible thing, an accident like that," the young doctor said, as we at last left the room. "Yet without it, we might have no opportunity to reach them with the Gospel."

"No Christian work is done up in the hills where they are?"

"I'm afraid not, especially with the present military situation.

"Now that these people have come down to the hospital, what are the chances?"

"Of conversion?"

I nodded.

"With the woman so severely injured, they are likely to be here for quite some time," Dr. Warlow said. "People like Emmy and Mrs. Mall witness to the patient."

"The others?" I asked, "The relatives? Will they attend the Gospel services?"

"Quite likely. Geoffrey has slide film showings, too, which the people enjoy."

He pointed across a segment of the hospital yard to what looked like a large billboard painted white for use as a projection screen.

"We are very careful in the way we present the Gospel," Dr. Warlow continued. "First of all, the Indian government frowns upon anyone suspected of what they call proselytizing."

"When I was in New Delhi a few days ago, arranging for permits to film *Tashi from Tibet,*" I told him, "I met with the head of the Division of External Affairs. He emphasized that India is a secular state, so far as its government is concerned, and that they frowned on proselytizing."

63

"Did you get any indication that he considered simply winning converts to be proselytizing?"

"At first this seemed to be the case," I replied. "In fact, it appeared we wouldn't get permission at all. It was pretty discouraging."

"So what happened?"

"I didn't quite know what to do, frankly, but I was determined to tell the truth. So I explained our purposes. I gave my own witness."

"What was the reaction?"

"He talked again about proselytizing. He said the government was eager to stamp out the kind of activity where an individual is promised personal gain in exchange for a confession of conversion."

"This has happened," the doctor said. "I suppose it still happens to a limited degree. How did he define personal gain?"

"He wasn't specific, except that he did mention students being sent to England and America for their education."

"Did he think you would do this type of thing?"

"I suppose. I told him we, as an organization, would not knowingly work with anyone who practiced economic proselytizing. Almost in an instant, his entire attitude changed. He said there were eight hundred thousand Buddhists in India before Independence. In the few years since then, the conversion of Hindus to Buddhism has brought this total to something like six million, I think he said. 'That's quite a lot of people getting converted!' he said quite jovially. And in the next five minutes, he told us we could secure whatever permits we needed."

"It's encouraging to hear this," Dr. Warlow said. "There are radical groups in India, the *Arya Samajists*, for example, a reformed cult of Hinduism, who become quite reactionary whenever anyone is converted to Christianity!"

"Do you see very many conversions?"

"Not nearly as many as we would like," the doctor answered. "For the most part, these are simple people; you know, country folk. They are very superstitious, deeply entrenched in the traditions of their religious backgrounds, and even though they may seem quite docile as you watch them here about the hospital, they can become terribly violent toward one of their group who makes a confession of having received Christ, especially if that person dares to allow himself to be baptised."

"Are there those who become secret believers?"

"Only God knows the answer to that. We do, from time to time, see indications that this has been the case."

We proceeded on now, to another private room where, in the next three days, I was to witness a pointed example of what we had been talking about.

The patient was a Muslim woman, a tetanus victim. As we entered, her husband, bearded and wearing the traditional black topi, stood to his feet.

Esther Kunz was in charge. The patient had been brought in during the night, and so once again it was a case of Miss Kunz foregoing sleep so that she might tend to one in critical need.

The windows were drawn, allowing only a

shaft of light into the room, and it took a moment for my eyes to acclimate. I could see well enough to watch the doctor examine the woman's chart. His face grew quickly taut.

"The spasms," he spoke softly, "increasing in intensity?"

Miss Kunz nodded.

He stepped to the bedside, and the wisp of a husband came quickly alongside.

I joined them.

"Notice the sardonic grin," the doctor said. He gripped the woman's chin, turning her face toward us, and I saw her face, like a caricature, eyes leering up at us, jaw set firm, and an eerie grin tight across her lips.

"What are her chances of survival?" I asked, being fully certain neither she nor her husband understood English."

"Very, very remote," Peter answered. "Tetanus is a terrible thing."

It was yet another scene to be always remembered. The doctor standing there. Miss Kunz ignoring her weariness. And the little husband, anxiously awaiting a word of hope from the doctor's lips.

"Isn't the husband unusual?" I whispered to Miss Kunz.

"In what way?" she asked.

"He seems so genuinely concerned about his wife."

"He shows real love for her."

"I had the idea this didn't often happen among Muslim men."

Our work has taken us frequently among Mohammedans. I was a guest on one occasion of a tribal chief on Bahrain Island in the Persian Gulf. On another occasion, Heinz Fussle and I were entertained by a prominent khan in Pakistan. We filmed a sequence for *The Harvester* in the courtyard of another wealthy khan, and the elated prince of Muslims insisted we be his guests for a meal. There have been other occasions, too, and in each of them we saw no women.

I remembered frequent conversations with a plastic surgeon, a missionary in Lahore, whose skill in nasal restoration had been enhanced by the nefarious trait of Pakistani men who, when displeased with a woman, would literally cut off her nose. I remembered too, reading such books as *Turtle Dove*, the story of a beautiful girl in North Africa and the cruelty of the husband her father had chosen.

But here, in this frightened husband, was an example of the other kind of Mohammedan man. His very manner revealed not only his gentleness, but the love he had shared with his wife.

"He stayed at her side all night," Miss Kunz told me.

"Are you able to talk to the woman?" I asked.

Miss Kunz nodded. "You pray for me," she said. "The husband also listens when I talk to the woman of Christ."

10 The hospital staff kept constant vigil at the Muslim woman's bedside, applying every known medical technique in a valiant effort to lift her strength above the infection's lethal grip. No hospital in America offers more conscientious care.

"Are there known cases of survival?" I

asked Dr. Warlow that evening, as we stopped in her room.

"Very rare," he said.

He took the woman's wrist, and the frightened little husband came a step closer. Patients who visit the hospital ascribe great power to the taking of the pulse beat, believing a doctor capable of detecting all manner of diseases simply by touching a sick person's wrist.

"Pulse is still quite good," he said, as he lowered the woman's arm to the bed. He took a moment to cover her arm, another gesture of kindness and concern so evident in the hospital. "But spasms are becoming worse and more frequent."

"There were several cases of what they called lock jaw in the small community where I lived as a boy," I said.

"Lock jaw. They call it that in America, too, do they?"

"Tetanus can enter through a very small wound, can't it?"

"It certainly can. One of the big problems is that so few of these people wear shoes. This woman stepped on a nail. Another problem is that the tetanus germ seems to thrive in these congested villages. Then, too, the soil having been tilled so many hundreds of years without rest, the fertility is badly spent. So, even if these people are able to raise enough food, there is a lack of proper nutrition. They simply don't develop any satisfactory resistance to disease!"

All during that next day, the woman lingered. Miss Kunz kept in close touch with her progress. "There's not much chance of saving her life," she told me, "but do pray that we will be able to win her soul."

"Are you making progress?"

"I've had some good talks with her."

"What's her response?"

"She's interested."

"Her husband?"

"He listens, too. I think they both realize the Christian faith offers them something they have both missed so far in their lives. So you pray."

I did pray, and in my intercession reaffirmed a spiritual law too seldom observed by today's Christians, the law of intercessory involvement, by which the mind and the hand project toward the point on which the heart is fixed.

My prayers for this woman turned my thoughts those next hours to the world of Islam.

Indeed, one cannot give a total consideration to modern India without thinking of Islam, since the tensions between India and Pakistan are essentially religious tensions. At Partition the state of Punjab was split between the two countries.

Herbertpur Hospital is near an area once part of the Punjab. Consequently, patients number an intermingling of Muslims and Hindus. Hindu villages predominate, but there are scattered Muslim villages and an occasional village where both religious groups live together.

Only on rare occasions does one hear of converts from Islam to the Christian faith. There have never been large scale conversions in any Islamic area, with the exception of a few places where the religion of Mohammed was implanted by Muslim missionaries.

I once visited a hospital within sight of

Saudi Arabia, the land of Mecca. Here the government is so frantically Muslim, Bibles are confiscated by customs officials, Arab soldiers stand outside the U.S. military base chapel to prevent citizens of the country from entering, and the Red Cross had to change its symbol to a red crescent. My travel associate and I spent many hours talking with the missionary staff, as they shared with us some of the treacherous aspects of their efforts to present Christ to people who so overtly disclaimed Him.

Earlier this same year, when we were in Pakistan filming *The Harvester*, I visited in the home of the head of an American mission, which had only recently held its annual field conference.

"We have fifty workers on the field," he told me, in answer to my question as to converts. "Through all our activities during the past twelve months, we were able to count some fifty-six souls who have given evidence of a real desire to make a spiritual decision. Of these fifty-six, we know of only eight outwardly living the Christian life."

I have heard Muslim students express interest in the Christian faith, and recall at least two such students who openly stated their conviction that the Christian faith is the true faith. Yet, even though I am told there are many such students in the world of Islam, no gem is more rare than the Muslim youth who will turn his back to the crescent so he may bow to the cross.

The convert to Christianity risks the fate of becoming a social leper, disinherited by his family, shunned by society. If he is married, his wife and children will be taken from him.

70

If he goes to the bazaar, or to the village shops, he cannot buy food. If he stops to drink at the village well, someone will spit into his cup or knock it from his hands. And if he dares to walk alone in lonely places or at night, he may lose his life.

As a private experiment, on occasions when I have had the opportunity to address church-related gatherings, I have asked those assembled to raise their hands if, any time during the previous six months, they have so much as once prayed for those who minister to the spiritual needs of Mohammedans.

When there is response, and often there is none, it rarely exceeds two percent of the number in attendance.

Remembering the law of intercessory involvement, it goes without saying that by far the vast populace of American Christians could hardly care less whether or not the courts of heaven will one day radiate with the countenance of those redeemed from within hearing distance of the Minaret.

Yet there are converts.

A missionary once told me of a man from Afghanistan, where life is of little value and where feuds go on from generation to generation, and where missionaries may not enter because the raging fires of fanticism run as rampant as they do across the sands approaching Mecca.

As some Afghans do, this man came down through the Khyber Pass into India, to barter his wares.

While in India, he fell ill and was taken to a mission hospital. Here, for the first time in his life, he heard the story of Golgotha, and the vacated tomb. The redeeming message fell upon good ground in his heart.

He professed the Christian faith.

As he was about to leave, the doctor in charge inquired as to his plans, to which the man replied, "I am going back to my village to tell my people what Christ has done for me, and what He can do for them."

Painfully aware of the high spiritual mortality among Muslims who return to their own kinsmen, the doctor counselled with the new convert, cautioned him about the opposition he was sure to encounter.

"My Lord hung upon the cross with all the sin of the world on His body," the Afghan said. "Surely He can give me strength to bear the reproach of the few men who live in my village."

So he went back. Back through the pass and up across the mountain trails to his home.

Because he was the son of a prominent family in the village, his first witness met with restrained opposition.

"Allah is one God," the local *Maulvi* told him, "and he never had a son." This is the crossroads at which the division between Islam and Christianity begins and widens.

The young man continued his witness. His people threatened him. If he continued his talk, they would stop him.

He continued.

So they laid hands on him and tied him to the ground and poured hot oil through his teeth searing the throat so that he lost his voice.

But he did not die.

When he was strong enough, he made the long trek back to the hospital once more. The mission doctor was able to bring his voice back to a whisper.

"It is all we can do," the doctor regretfully informed the patient. "You can never speak normally again."

"Then I will go back and whisper about Jesus," the man avowed.

And he did.

He returned to his village, and was never again seen by the people at the hospital. Quite sometime later, the report came of his martyrdom. It was said to have happened when he repeatedly refused to keep silent and his own brothers nailed him to a cross in the heart of their village. There they left him to hang until dead.

I thought again and again of instances like this, as I watched Dr. Warlow and Miss Kunz struggle to save the life of the tetanus patient. And as Miss Kunz told of the imperiled woman's open heart to her Christian witness.

In conversations with members of the hospital staff, I learned that Herbertpur had its own snatched firebrands.

In 1946, a young girl came to the hospital. It was the day before Christmas. She listened to the singing. She took in every word of the preaching. She opened her heart.

One day, as the Bible woman sat talking nearby, the name of Jesus came into the conversation.

"Isn't it a beautiful name?" the girl interrupted. "I love to hear it."

The sincerity of that love became evident some days later when, due to the nature of her illness, the medical staff told her she would need to go to a larger hospital for treatment.

"But cannot God heal me?" she asked.

Then, at her request, staff members gathered about her bed to pray for her healing.

The prayer was answered.

Instead of going to the larger hospital, she returned to her village, but only to come soon again to the hospital with her mother and two of her sisters who, so impressed by what had happened in the girl's life, asked if they, too, might hear the words of Jesus.

During the time of the Partition, when India's Sikhs led the blood purge against Muslims living in the East of the then Punjab, several examples of Christian witness and provision took place in the area of the hospital, the more remarkable when one visits a few of these villages and, by human equation, realizes how infinitesimal is the breakthrough of the Christian message into the great wall of religious prejudice, be it Muslim or Hindu.

The Mohammedan girl, who received Christ at the hospital and then trusted Him to heal her body, later died in childbirth.

A year after the girl's death, her mother, who had come to the hospital at her daughter's insistence to hear the Christian message, and had subsequently opened her own heart to that message, made a return visit to Herbertpur.

In a moment of sadness, she recounted the death of her daughter, but the light returned to her eyes as she told of the spiritual peace in her daughter's heart.

The mother recounted the power of God in her own life, and especially of the time when, in the heat of the Partition uprising, avenging Hindus marched from village to village, killing every Muslim in their path.

Members of this woman's family were terrified, but did not know where to go for safety.

"Stay right here in our village," she told

them. "The Lord Jesus Christ looks over us, and He will keep us safe."

Although the Hindus sacked every village around them, this woman's village was left untouched. It is a miracle spoken of to this day by the people of the area.

Even at the heat of the uprisings, the hospital vehicle could go from Muslim villages to Hindu, and from Hindu villages to Muslim, and at all times unscathed, so complete was the confidence of all the people in the goodness of the foreigners at Herbertpur.

In talking with people, such as those at the hospital who minister to Muslims, one often hears the term "secret believer."

I remember the account of one man who considered Christ's claim upon his life for several years before he knocked one night on the door of a missionary's house, and announced his readiness to at last become a believer.

Because of his prominence, he escaped outright physical molestation. Persecution came in other ways, however. He was scorned. His wife turned against him. Pressure was brought upon his business. He was left friendless and alone.

At last he came to the missionary and, weeping, said, "I can endure it no longer, Sahib. I must be honest and tell you. I have begun to go once again to the mosque at the time of prayer, for this is what my brothers say I must do to regain their favor. Please do not turn against me and say I am no longer a follower of Christ. While the others bow in prayer to Allah, I cry out to my Living Redeemer. And when they recite the words of the Koran, I repeat the twenty-third Psalm."

Dr. Lehmann enjoys telling of a man who

worked for his wife's family when she lived as a child in India. Hearing of her return, he asked if he might work in the Lehmann household.

Outwardly, he was a Muslim. Yet he took great delight in going with the Lehmanns from village-to-village, selling Christian literature.

A Hindu man in the area had a dream, in which he sat at the back of a dark cave and watched a man, seated in a circle of light at the front of the cave, reading a book.

"The meaning of the dream is plain," the supposed Mohammedan said. "You, because you are an unbeliever, are the man sitting in the darkness. The man sitting in the light is our Doctor Sahib, who has come to India to show the way out of evil darkness. If you will listen to the words Doctor Sahib reads from the Bible, you will be saved from your sins."

Because of this witness, the man came to Dr. Lehmann, and as a consequence of their discussions, became a believer.

I have talked with Christians in this part of the world who feel the church is on the verge of significant spiritual breakthrough among the Muslims, some insisting this break-through would readily occur if the Christian church involved itself in a real concern for its harvestlands.

If Christians would experience intercessory involvement!

Or could it be that, irrespective of the calloused souls of homeland Christians, whenever the Gospel is proclaimed among Muslims, there will always be fruit? Perhaps not fruit which fits the description of our own evangelical nomenclature, but genuine fruit all the same. So, in the beakers of honest analysis, there may be little difference between the Christian in America, who proclaims his faith without committing his life, and the frightened Muslim who hides his faith in silence.

Innumerable American Christians have invested their years in material abundance and then, stepping into the twilight, have looked back in bitter repentance upon years of spiritual wasteland. So, too, it may well be that men, whom the world has called Muslims, will at the moment of death fix their eyes upon a glimmer of comprehensible Light and, equally justified, join the throngs of redeemed at the Savior's throne.

There was Light in the room of the tetanus patient at Herbertpur, and we all prayed earnestly for the penetration of that Light into the gathering darkness.

The tetanus patient died.

When Miss Kunz came to the house to tell us, her face was drawn in disappointment and weariness, but there was a touch of warmth to her eyes.

So I asked, "Did she believe before she died?"

"I think so," Miss Kunz said. "When I first told her how serious her case was, she was quite frightened. Then we talked of God's greatness. Being a Muslim, she, of course, believed in God."

"Had she ever heard the Gospel?" I asked.

The nurse shook her head. "But she listened as I told her. She was quite uncomfortable, and the spasms left her weak, but she seemed to try very hard to understand what I was saying. Then last night, after one of the worst spasms, she looked at me and said she would soon be going home. 'I don't mean my village home,' she said, 'I mean the home God has for me.'"

"You think she understood her need of salvation?"

"It's hard to say, but I feel she did. There was such a victorious spirit in the room. It seemed the very forces of evil had been driven out. I carefully explained to her what Christ had done for her on the cross, and she eagerly drank in every word. Then, just shortly before she died, she said something very unusual."

"What was that?"

"Her husband was standing beside me, and she looked up at both of us and said, 'Jesus and *Bhagwan* are the same.'"

"*Jesus and Bhagwan* are the same?" I repeated, wondering.

"What I think she was trying to tell me was that all her life she had been seeking for God. Perhaps, when she heard the word *Bhagwan*, which the Hindus use, she may have wondered if He might be the one who could bring her to a real knowledge of spiritual truth."

Across my mind swept the Biblical quotation, *In the beginning was the Word*.

The early Greeks had had their problems with spiritual darkness. Somewhere, undefined and beyond their power to designate, was *the Logos*. John had spoken of *the Logos*, in proclaiming to the world that Christ alone fulfills man's spiritual search.

"We must pray for this woman's husband," Miss Kunz continued. "He loved his wife very much, and he was so impressed by the peacefulness of her death that it almost kept him from showing any sorrow."

All that day, and many times thereafter, I thought about that woman.

Suppose there had been no hospital at Herbertpur, no missionary nurse to give physical comfort while she told of a Savior's eternal love?

Then there would only have been *Bhagwan* and darkness, darkness and fear, and an unprepared entry beyond the great fixed gulf.

I remembered flying across India at low altitude in a twin engine plane, which gave me a sweeping view of the hundreds of villages below. I remembered how my heart ached, realizing most of the villages I saw had never had a Christian witness because there was no hospital, no mission station, nothing.

But there *is* a witness at Herbertpur.

Why?

Why here but not in multitudes of other places whose need is as great?

I had to find the answer. For I was convinced that, in finding the answer, I would look fully into the embarrassed countenance of an entity called the Church which, after two thousand years, seems not to believe that the only hindrance to the building of a Herbertpur wherever it is needed across the world is the absence of belief itself!

11 Since no one lives long enough to come to a full knowledge of himself, no point is gained in trying to conjecture how long it would take to become fully acquainted with another human being.

Any biographical attempt, be the subject

contemporary or historical, faces the immediate premise of the biographer's own personality and prejudices. A college professor of mine once said there are now as many Napoleons as there are books written about him.

In addition to this is the fact that, however much source material a writer may have at his disposal, he can hope to do little more than peer between the covers of the real story of a man's life. He can only write what he sees or, more accurately, what he thinks he sees.

In the case of an individual no longer living, the biographer is left with second-hand source material at best, plus his own imagination. Neither of which can be called true documentation. Fortunately, biographer Parson Weems lived long enough to admit that, lacking in source material on the boyhood of George Washington, he invented the episode about chopping down the cherry tree.

In the four or five short weeks I spent with Dr. Geoffrey Lehmann, I could scarcely get to know him. Looking back, it continues to amaze me that so busy a man could find so much time to assist me in my search for material. This is one of his gifts, the ability to be so engrossed in work at one moment, so completely relaxed and at ease in another.

It would be folly for me to claim knowledge in depth of the good doctor. What I can say, however, is that I observed principles of stewardship and dedication unique and refreshing in this kind of world. I feel certain the more one learned of the man and his ministry, the more vividly these principles would be illustrated.

What stays with me more than any other single factor, however, is the memory of the spirit permeating so much I observed at the hospital. This spirit, this obvious outgrowing of dedicated talent and right principle, brought to my heart the growing and compelling conviction to do what I could in making known what I had experienced at Herbertpur.

Several days went by, however, before I felt the opportune time had come to again broach the subject. That time came one evening, just before dinner, when the doctor invited me to walk with him in the garden.

If to leave the dusty road and enter the hospital compound is like suddenly being taken from India to another part of the world, then a walk through the doctor's garden is like closing one's eyes to pain and confusion and frustration and human inequities and all but the contemplation of goodness and beauty and serenity.

"I can't spend nearly as much time as I would like in the garden," he said, "but, even so, it is a wonderful respite to be able to get away here for a few moments."

He pointed to various plantings, some of them familiar, but most unknown to me. His special interest seems to be trees, both fruit bearing and decorative. As we came alongside a small lime, he chuckled and said, "This is the tree that gave us Englishmen our special name here in India. They often call us Limeys, you know."

"I've heard of the English being called Limeys," I said, "but wasn't aware of the derivation."

"When the English first came to India, they resorted to limeade as a source of comfort from the extreme heat. The Indians, who already had all kinds of interesting names for us, added this to their list."

The Lehmanns have imported from England a home device for water carbonation, which gives an added zest to the garden's supply of citrus juices.

"This part of India has an abundance of beautiful trees, for which we are most grateful," he continued. "The most beautiful of all, I think, is acacia japonica, covered from March to August with a yellow and pink double blossom which is like a waterfall of beauty. We also have the flame of the forest in the jungles. It comes at the start of the hot season. The trees, together with the heat, give the illusion that the whole forest is on fire."

He named others. A tree called the nugo mora. Another named gold mohr.

As he talked on, at times philosophical, then with something of the spirit of the poet, then simply as a man of leisure, my thoughts turned to the compulsion so strong in my heart.

So, as we came off the path and onto the lawn, toward the water lily bed directly out from my bedroom window, I bluntly asked, "Have you come to any decision as to our proposed project?"

We paused by a bed of cannas, stopping to pluck weed sprouts the gardener had missed. "I have given it a lot of thought," he said. "What you say about sharing one's testimony with others."

He stood, shook the dirt from the weed roots, tossed them aside. "I have one problem," he said.

"What is it?" I asked.

"When I was a boy, many missionaries visited our home in England. I got the impression they were examples of spiritual perfection. I was not very long in India, though, until I discovered a missionary is one of Satan's choice targets. Looking back across the thirty years since we first came here, I am of the opinion that becoming a missionary is the one career most likely to bring out all of a man's faults and weaknesses."

"Sounds like great copy for a book!" I primed.

He looked at me strangely. Then he smiled and said, "Maybe that's my problem. Maybe I'm afraid if you put me down in writing, my faults will come out for permanent viewing."

"When they are honestly admitted, and counter-balanced by his virtues, a man's faults can give encouragement and strength to others," I said.

"I suppose so."

He thought a moment. "Pride is one fault with which I have struggled the hardest. It has been a real discipline in my life to at least try to conduct myself so that the Lord, not I, gets the glory for whatever may be accomplished through my efforts."

"More good copy," I said, realizing as soon as I had spoken that I was being a bit too jovial for the situation.

But the good doctor has a boundless sense of humor, which his children say has a schoolboy characteristic, and so he countered by saying, "I must be careful, or you will talk me into this affair in spite of all my humility!"

"Humility is simply the art of being honest," I said.

He grew serious now. "As you know, my mother lies buried in the little cemetery beside the chapel. After my father died, she

83

came out and spent the winter with us, intending to go home. Father had always been responsible for the men servants, the butler and the chauffeur, and we wondered how she would manage. But she never got back to England. She just quietly slipped away, while here with us.

"It was perhaps fitting this way, as I had always been a special pet of hers. It was often quite embarrassing, even as a very young child, when she would boast of me in the presence of others. I became something of a mama's boy, you might say. On the one hand, I relished her praise of me, but at the same time her doting attitude had the traumatic effect of causing me to become quite introverted.

"I felt everything I did must be perfect, and it crushed me to have anyone criticize what I had done. To this day, I'm much too inclined to worry about what people will think of me and my work. As a child, I often took to sulking and temperamental outbursts. All because of pride, of course. I'm afraid some of this came with me to the mission field, and it has only been after much prayer and taking daily inventory that the Lord has seen fit to give me at least a measure of victory.

"So you see, I'm being quite honest when I say I must be careful about this matter of publicity."

"You understand," I said, "that I have no inclination for publicity as such. God uses people as His instruments. People motivate people. This is what interests me about your story."

"I discussed your suggestion with Monica. She's been a wonderful help to me all these years, especially when it comes to determining the fine points of the Lord's will. You speak of honesty. That's one word that most accurately characterizes my dear wife."

"What does she say?" I asked.

"We both are anxious for every opportunity to make known the ministry here at Herbertpur. Because of the nature of our work, our coming unsponsored to India, we really suffer in the fact that so few people know us and, consequently, so few pray. For this reason, both Monica and I would be quite happy if something could be written about Herbertpur, but without us being prominent in it."

"That," I commented, "would be like writing a book on England's role in World War II, but omitting the name Winston Churchill!"

He didn't seem convinced.

So I added. "You are concerned lest people get the idea the hospital has succeeded because of you rather than because of God's blessing."

"That's our very great concern."

"Can you not see real blessing coming, however, from a book on the hospital here which shows what God has done through you?"

"If this could be done with such clarity that no one, reading the book, would have any question but what the ministry is of the Lord, not of us."

"This would certainly be my objective."

"But there are many missionary hospitals. Why choose this one?"

"For several reasons. First, the incidents which led me to Herbertpur. As I'm sure you do, Dr. Lehmann, my daily prayer is for the Holy Spirit to lead me into purposeful contacts. Life passes so quickly, making it all the more important that each event of life be utilized in the fullest possible measure for God's glory. But there is an even more impelling reason."

"What is that?"

"You have a unique message for the Christian world."

"A message?"

"Back in America, interest in the church per se is at an all time high. More even than during the war years, I would think. But, for most Christians, the Christian faith has not touched their pocketbooks. In fact, you talk about stewardship to the average American Christian, and he throws up a wall of resistance. The collection plate is a favorite subject for jokes."

He gave me his complete attention now, and hope rose in my heart.

"Nuclear fallout has spiritual as well as human significance. In many cases without knowing it, I'm sure, people have migrated back to the church . . . that is, the physical church . . . because they feel they need God. Not at the center of their lives, of course, not as a motivating force in what they do, but they want to be sure God is within reach. At any moment, some dictator may go berserk and plunge the world into chaos, and in that event, God will be expected to move in and handle the situation. His special blessings will, of course, fall first of all upon those who have favored Him by their occasional presence in church.

"The example of your stewardship, the willingness of you and your wife to invest your personal wealth as you have done, in my opinion, this is one of the exciting events in the history of missions."

"But we dare not imply that money, in itself, is a success factor in Christian service."

"I'm not sure I agree," I said. "This is something I've given a great deal of personal thought. There is a sacred aspect to money. True, as the Bible says, *the love of money is the root of all evil,* but money, actually, is the result of the combination of our talents and the time and energy expended to properly utilize these talents. In a sense, money is the very fruit of life. It's a principle of stewardship, the willingness to work hard to earn money and the application of God-given wisdom to properly use money.

"Now, of course," I continued, "in a strict sense of the word, you are right. Money is not the basic issue in Christian service. The basic issues are personal motivations, making sure of I Cor. 10:31 functioning in every part of what we are and do.

"And when the motivations are right, economics are also right. A man's first thought is not to be sure his standard of living equals his income, but that, to the fullest possible extent, his income is being used to further Christ's cause on earth.

"Your story, Dr. Lehmann . . . the example of your stewardship . . . if this could be brought to the attention of thinking Christians back in America . . ."

From inside the house came the sound of the great gong announcing dinner. We moved toward the front veranda, the doctor setting the pace with reflective, measured steps.

As we came up onto the veranda, he said, "Suppose we get together right after evening prayers. You perhaps would like to ask questions. You may just discover that I am quite a commonplace subject, and decide not to pursue your thought of a book any further."

Mealtime with the Lehmanns is always a pleasant adventure. The fine Christian cook, in consultation with Mrs. Lehmann and with quite some help from the good doctor as well, puts out a fare that is both ingenious and delectable. Ingenious because this is India, where the killing of cattle is a criminal offense, and the Lehmanns are blessed with a cook who has the unique ability of making pork taste like beef. Delectable because, as respite from the demanding rigors of the day, food is always prepared with the thought of adding a touch of relaxed delight to the appeasement of hunger.

Because the food was so interesting, my wife asked me to keep notes, sending home in my letters to her examples of pleasant menus. But I am at a loss to say what was served that night, or how it tasted, so high had anticipation risen in my heart for the telling of the doctor's story.

12 Following prayers and the day's last spot of tea, Mrs. Lehmann retired to the drawing room to write letters, the doctor selected some music for the record player, and we settled back to talk.

Through the years, it has often been my privilege to interview outstanding Christians and, subsequently, prepare short sketches for magazine publication. With rare exception, the lives of these people have mundane beginings.

Not so Geoffrey Lehmann.

He was born in mid-January, at about the turn of the century, near historic Alexandra Palace in London. As a child, he often watched the Queen's servants at their tasks on the grounds, and caught occasional glimpses of royalty.

Though the place of residence bore a London address, it lay far enough toward the country for the Lehmanns to enjoy a few touches of agrarian life. They had chickens, ducks, turkeys, as well as cows, pigs and goats. And ponies for the children to ride.

Directly to the back of the house was a field, and just beyond this a sprawling forest where Manny, the governess, frequently took the children. The ponies and the dogs simplified the imaginative progress of turning the woods into Sherwood Forest, the little field and residential compound to an enchanting Nottingham.

They also had a country place at Bevan, a greystone cottage built in the sixteenth century and surrounded by the storied moors, wide and verdant wonderlands for play. A little stream ran nearby, and here the family improvised a swimming pool by building a small dam.

So the world was a friendly place for the boy Geoffrey, and nature became an early friend.

"My parents were very wise," the doctor recalls. "As best they could, they filled our lives with wholesome experiences. I remember so well back home in London how, every Saturday afternoon, we children watched the chauffeur as he fired up our steam-driven family car. It took thirty minutes, and we watched every stage of the procedure with keen interest. The chauffeur lit the various jets, which burned kerosene, and little by little as the water began to boil the car made a most intriguing sound. We loved it."

Once the quaint vehicle had built up a sufficient head of steam, the children got in and they headed out for a pleasant spin through Epping Forest. The car made a chugging sound as it rumbled along. Occasional stops had to be made at wayside cottages when the boiler ran low on water.

With a bit of urging, the chauffeur would venture on to a stretch of straightway at the plodding top speed of thirty miles an hour. There would be occasional stops at little shops along the forest road for biscuits and tea.

"On these trips to the forest, I discovered my first love for trees," the doctor says, "especially the birch with it's silver bark."

While Monica Lehmann is as obviously British as the roll of the letter R, the more I observed her husband during those days at the hospital, the more I suspected he might have European heritage a bit closer than the flow of the Thames to my own Scandinavian progenitors. Even the name Lehmann did not seem to ring completely British, though I am by no means a student of family names.

So I was not surprised, in our discussion that evening, to hear that the grandfather had come to England from Cologne, Germany.

Blessed with the breath of genius, he could sit at his drawing board around the clock, designing improvements for industrial machines, but he lived in the ominous days of Bismarck. The war with Denmark and Austria, the diplomatic game of tic-tac-toe with France, the famed *Kulturkampf*, these had brought German military conscription, based on the assumption that every man must learn to fight.

Although in no sense a pacifist, the young inventor detected the seeds of doom in Germany's rising militarism, so he drew up his stakes and migrated to England. He was by no means a man of wealth, but was able to bring with him sufficient funds to set up a small workshop.

The young immigrant's skill came to the attention of government authorities, who commissioned him to design the lathes to cut the new British association thread, a phase of the government's efforts toward standardization. The project succeeded so well that Mr. Lehmann set up a small factory, which he eventually turned over to his two sons, Ernest and Samuel.

Samuel Lehmann, Geoffrey's father, subsequently purchased full interest in the enterprise.

As is so often the case with inventors, it appears Grandfather Lehmann was too taken with the pursuit of craftsmanship to concern himself much about the pursuit of money. Consequently, son Samuel lacked capitalization when he took over the business, and spent the early years of his marriage in the demoralizing struggle of pitting accounts payable versus accounts receivable.

Because of his tenacious spirit, Samuel Lehmann was destined to succeed. However, the affluence which surrounded young Geoffrey's childhood came largely from his mother, a

91

woman twenty-eight years of age when she married Samuel, six years her junior. Her age, together with her material means, tended to give her the dominant voice in the family. Then, too, the father worked hard in the business, many times laboring through the night, and was consequently unable to give full attention to his family.

What the Lehmanns' side may have lacked in pounds sterling, it made up with abundance in mental acumen and manual artistry — the grandfather with his creative genius, the grandmother with exceptional talent in music.

"All of my father's family were wonderful musicians," the doctor remembers. "I would sometimes sit for hours listening to Granny Lehmann at the keyboard."

Young Geoffrey's parents belonged to the "exclusive" segment of the Plymouth Brethren. So exclusive, in fact, that the doctor remembers meetings with no more than six people in attendance. Fine Christians, he recalls, but with a tenaciously separatist outlook on the rest of Christianity.

Young Geoffrey attended a prep school run by a strict adherent of this group. However limited his ecclesiastical horizons might have been, however, the schoolmaster counterbalanced this with a boundless interest in the modern world.

Few years had passed since Wilhelm Röntgen's discovery of the X-Ray. It was one of the marvels of the day, an awesome eye fashioned by the art of science. Mr. Brown, the schoolmaster, demonstrated the wonders of the new discovery, young Geoffrey listening in wide-eyed wonder, even though he could not at that time have had the slightest thought of a career in medicine.

Mr. Brown developed a machine, run by electricity, which produced a shower of big, cascading sparks. He had a flair for the dramatic, and used such contraptions to stimulate the minds of his students to an appreciation and a curiosity for the many wonders of the world.

Staid though the schoolmaster may have appeared to be in his theological persuasions, the time came when his zest for the wonders of science lay bare a point of weakness. The Brethren, of course, decried all forms of worldly amusement, including the fledgling cinema, but one day, in the sheer enthusiasm for science, Mr. Brown invited a man with a moving picture projector to give the children a demonstration.

It was the year 1913, and as the windows of the little schoolroom were darkened, the screen and projector set in place, Geoffrey and his classmates waited in hushed entrancement for the beginning of the performance.

"Children," Mr. Brown introduced, "in 1824, a man by the name of Peter Mark Roget read a paper to the Royal Society in England titled "The Persistance of Vision with Regard to Moving Objects." Among those present were Sir John Herschel, and Michael Faraday, who were so inspired by Mr. Roget's paper they began various experimental investigations. Sometime later, on the continent, Dr. Joseph Antoine Plateau and Dr. Simon Ritter developed a method for viewing a series of still pictures, each representing a phase of motion, so that the illusion of movement occurred. Then, about nineteen years ago, the American inventor, Thomas Edison, developed the kinescope. What you are seeing today results from the dedicated efforts of these men to advance this new scientific achievement."

Having thus so eruditely set the stage for the display of scientific phenomenon, Mr. Brown sat down, folded his arms, and waited in smiling contentment for the beginning of the presentation.

His composure endured but for a moment.

As the man with the machine began turning the handle, transporting the film behind the lens, a bevy of dancing girls leaped onto the screen, their gyrations given a visual pizzicato effect by the choppy movement of the aperture.

"Stop! Stop!" Mr. Brown demanded, rushing horrified to the projector.

The PB background, while it did introduce a goodly share of negatives into the young boy's life, abundantly counterbalanced these with the knowledge and the respect he developed for the Bible and the Christian faith.

"Mr. Brown was an excellent teacher," the doctor told me, "and made sure we kept our lessons in the best of the British tradition. He also organized his teaching so that we had time for Bible study and scripture memorization."

Again and again, during discussions at family devotions, Geoffrey would surprise his parents by answering some scriptural question. When asked how he had learned this, he invariably replied, "Oh, Mr. Brown."

Gospel services were also held at the school, and as a result of one such service, the young lad began to seriously ponder his own spiritual circumstances.

"I was nine years of age," he remembers, "and as we boys lined up two by two after the service, I kept asking myself whether I had really trusted in Jesus Christ. Right there where I stood, without anyone at the time knowing my thoughts, I asked God to make me His child, and in that moment, I knew He had answered my prayer."

So explicit had been the delineation of the scriptures to children reared and educated in God-fearing Plymouth Brethren surroundings!

From this school, he took an entrance exam for a public school in London. It was at this time when the father introduced the incentive of economic gain into the pursuit of learning. Geoffrey had been consistently in the bottom twenty-five percent of the class, until his father offered him two and sixpence if he emerged to the top one-fourth.

School work had always come easy, he was the family intellectual, but it took this added incentive from his father to bring the lad's mental prowess into full display.

He not only moved quickly to the top twenty-five percent, but was eventually one of the top three. This classroom prowess, more than anything else, set him up on the pedestal of his mother's special favor.

"Have you met my boy Geoffrey?" "Have you heard how well Geoffrey did at school?" "Come, Geoffrey, these people would like to see my nice, bright boy." Though perhaps well-intentioned, these parental plaudits did the lad little, if any, good. His natural shyness increased. At the numerous and large family gatherings, he often found excuse to keep out of view, much to his mother's consternation. Thus came into large blight a lifelong inferiority complex, a weakness he has learned to shield with considerable adroitness.

"I had an innocent and inquiring mind," he said. "I was especially sensitive to nature, with all its beauty and wonder. Without the slightest intention of being risqué, I provided quite a shock on one occasion with an essay I wrote about sparrows, in which I mentioned that two sparrows lived together and, as a result, the eggs hatched."

The Plymouth Brethren did more than provide Geoffrey Lehmann with a Biblical basis for his life. His father took him one year to Fenton, where he met several other young people, one a young girl in whom his brother showed particular interest.

These young people, though Plymouth Brethren, did not believe in exclusive meetings. They were what has come to be known as the Open Brethren, the public being allowed to attend their worship gatherings.

"I remember when we returned to London," the doctor mused, "and we went back to our regular meeting. Our father was told that, if he would agree the table where he had met and taken communion with the Open Brethren was the table of the devil, he would be restored to fellowship. Otherwise, he should no longer meet with our group. As a result of this, we left the exclusive Brethren, and met after that with the Open Brethren, with whom we had very happy fellowship."

Rapport with the Open Brethren became the portal to multiple opportunities and blessings for the maturing young Lehmann.

England has its Children's Special Service Mission, a highly-respected and well known youth evangelism function better known as the CSSM, and Geoffrey assisted his brother in services.

One summer, they held CSSM meetings at a seaside resort, and often walked the beach inviting young people to attend. On one such day, Geoffrey came upon a widowed mother and her daughters basking in the sun.

"Pardon me, Madam," Geoffrey interposed politely, "but I wonder if your daughters would like to attend the CSSM meeting we are holding this evening."

A chatter of enthusiastic assent came from the daughters, explained by the mother who told Geoffrey she and the girls were believers, and had been hoping for an opportunity to fellowship with other Christians during their holiday.

Geoffrey scarcely noticed a charming lass, just twelve years of age so at this point in life much younger than he, but all the same that first meeting with the Allen family, and especially with petite Monica Allen, was to have lifelong significance.

Monica was quiet, with a sensitive spirit much like his own. She spent long hours reading, and was often so quiet in the presence of others as to be unnoticed. Even as a twelve-year-old, she dreamed of returning to India, the land of her birth, as a missionary. It was of little more than passing interest to Geoffrey, who did think of sometime visiting India as a tourist, but nothing more.

Yet there was a magnetism between them. Monica matured quickly and ere long the short spread of years between them became of no consequence. So the two of them grew to be good friends, and often spent long periods of time in discussion as visits between the Lehmann and Allen families became more frequent.

"At first," the doctor remembers, "we were more like brother and sister. She would often come to me for advice. There were times when she became quite discouraged, perhaps for no reason in particular, and I being the optimistic type would be able to help her. Throughout our lives, we have balanced each other in many ways. I am the one to jump at things, and she tends to be more careful. The Lord has used these different traits to bring each of our lives into better balance."

Christian workers often came to stay with the Lehmanns, one of the most memorable being a hulking Norwegian who charmed the children by eating his breakfast of fried eggs with neither the use of a knife nor a fork.

"Praise the Lord, Madam," he exuded to the somewhat abashed hostess, "I am glad you have an iron bedstead."

Mrs. Lehmann, it so happens, was rather proud of the fine brasswork of the bed the evangelist had occupied, and was not particularly pleased to have it spoken of as iron construction.

"Last place I stayed," the evangelist continued, "they put me in a wooden bed, and in the middle of the night it busted down under my weight."

Not all of the itinerants were quite this crude, but there were enough of this stripe to convince Geoffrey he wanted no part of vocational Christian service.

It was the loquacious Scandinavian who,

thinking to be funny, pushed the Lehmann's dog into a decorative pool just outside their house. "People like this became very offensive to me," the doctor says, "and I had a tendency to relate them with many other Christian workers who, no doubt, were good people."

Then, too, there were those who insisted on delivering lengthy preachments to the children, no doubt supposing it to be their duty, and not realizing the negative thrust of their conduct upon young and formative minds.

Missionaries also frequented the home, and these young Geoffrey observed with special interest. They seemed to be a species set apart. Not so much by their appearance and activity, perhaps, as by the fuss that was made over them when they came.

"Quite early in my childhood," the doctor relates, "I determined not to be a missionary."

Although never outwardly rebelling at the social confinement imposed by the religious convictions of his parents, a certain amount of inflicted trauma resulted to plague his maturing years.

"I saw basic genuineness in my parents and their Christian friends," he told me, "and the foundational concepts of my life follow the pattern of their convictions. I have come to feel, however, that it is not wise to shelter children from the world without giving them something more than a negative basis for abstinence."

Unfortunately, this sheltering involved not only a complete break with the world, as the elder Lehmanns understood it, but it also included, as has so often been the case with

Christian parents, almost complete negligence in helping children understand the awakening life surges within themselves.

"I must have been eighteen years of age," the doctor says, "when I was dissecting a female rabbit in a biology laboratory, and became greatly shocked and embarrassed to discover that animals had such things as ovaries and eggs. This amused my colleagues and added to my frustrations.

"And yet I am very reluctant to criticize my parents. They were so very sincere in their Christian lives, and any fault they may have had in their responsibilities to me must have resulted from previous failures on the part of their own parents."

Through the encouragement of his parents, he became increasingly active in the CSSM and at one of these youth meetings, as a teenager, he felt constrained to tell God his life was completely at His disposal.

"At the time," he remembers, "I had not the slightest inclination that this meant anything more than the fulfillment of my dream to go into business with my father."

By now the father had built the factory into a public company, destined to become the largest of its kind in Great Britain. Young Geoffrey Lehmann envisioned himself as one of England's young men of note, an integral part of a corporation with headquarters in London and factories all over the world.

It was a bright future. It quickened his step and caused him to hold his head high, charging his mind with enthusiasm as he made plans to enter Oxford University.

13 Oxford.
Legend dates it back to Brutus and the Druids.

Once primarily a school of letters, enshrining such alumni as Roger Bacon, Erasmus, Wycliff and Sir Thomas More, Oxford kept pace with the world, adding new schools of higher learning in compliance with man's need.

New facilities for engineering, opened in 1912, awaited Geoffrey Lehmann's enrollment.

It could scarcely have concerned him less that at St. Giles' Gate, a short distance from the main cluster of colleges, stood the Eye Hospital to which students of the healing arts came from all over the world.

No, Geoffrey Lehmann would be an engineer. It was in his blood. It was the first quest of his eyes as he observed the structure of a new building or admired the Houses of Parliament or Canterbury Cathedral or London Bridge. Engineers gave man the good things of life. They made possible his fine sports car, a gift from his father, identical in design to the vehicle presently holding the world's record. Engineers were the tall men of earth, the clever and the strong, and he was one with them.

He took his bachelor of science degree in civil and mechanical engineering, later doing research work in high frequency fatigue of metals.

"Metal can stand a stress of so many tons per square inch," he explained to me, "but when these metals are subjected to continued strain for a given period, the metal will break at a much lower stress than the initial maximum. This test is normally done at two thousand revolutions per minute, with a curve to show the highest limit to which a given metal can be subjected without breaking."

During this time, airplanes were being developed to travel at high speeds, and engineers were asking whether breaks would occur more quickly at a lower stress if the tension were applied more rapidly. What would happen, for example, if these stresses were put on at twenty thousand rpm instead of the customary two thousand?

"I was able to design a machine which put stresses up to fifty times per square inch, and compression up to as many times as twenty thousand revolutions per second. This showed that the fatigue of these metals, when tested at very high speed, was much more than the normal fatigue limit."

The cost of Geoffrey's research was underwritten by the Royal Aeronautical Society, and the paper later published by them, a part of his doctorate thesis.

The integrity of the Lehmann spiritual background was validated again and again during those days at Oxford, as Geoffrey added new spiritual dimensions to his academic pursuits.

He discovered, for example, that the Christian student organization on campus was in the hands of mere formalists, with no real concern for spiritual vitality.

Concerned, Geoffrey got together with a couple of other students, and discussed possible procedures. What should they do? Quietly withdraw and leave the status quo undisturbed, or make an effort to take a hand in repairing the situation?

102

Courage is at times a scarce human commodity, especially among Christians when wrongs need to be righted. In this respect, however, young Mr. Lehmann showed the colors which were later to carry him halfway across the world, to face a multitude of unknowns.

"Let's talk with the leaders of the Union," he suggested. "Maybe they will listen to reason."

So an approach was made.

When stiff resistance met the suggestions for change, Geoffrey and his friends organized the Evangelical Union, a student function which continues its effective ministry among students at Oxford.

"It was very difficult for us," he recalls. "Many said we were harming the total effect of Christian witness on campus. But time has dealt favorably with us, and has shown that, whereas we may not have been fully mature in our judgements and procedures, the basis of our thinking was right. As I look back now, I can see the reason. We prayed earnestly that God would show us what to do."

Strongly contributing to the liberalization of student Christian activity was the appearance of famed Mr. Buchman, apostle of Moral Rearmament, whose global movement began on the Oxford campus and came to be known, among other things, as the Oxford Movement. Overt pressure came upon the Evangelical Union to disband and become part of this promised new utopia.

"At that time," the doctor says, "we knew nothing about Buchman or his movement. We wanted to be part of whatever God was doing on campus, and certainly not to in any way hinder His work. I remember how several of us met and spent much time praying for the Lord's will. The more we prayed, asking God to guide us, the less sure we became that Buchman's philosophy was sound."

The doctor especially remembers one meeting, addressed by a prominent British general who had been swept up by the Moral Rearmament concept.

"Why did you not once mention the name of Christ?" Geoffrey asked after the lecture.

"It is our method of approaching spiritual truth," the general managed to say, though taken somewhat off-guard. "We gradually lead up to this."

Geoffrey attended a number of subsequent sessions, but when no Christian emphasis was forthcoming, he and his friends saw no alternative but to boycott the movement as a form of clever apostasy.

"In later years," he told me, as we discussed the Oxford era of his life, "Buchman's followers seem to have put some emphasis on Christ. I wonder, though, if it is not at best thinking of Christ philosophically and not as Lord and Savior. Satan is so clever. His devices are not all dark and sinister. He can also lead men into false light, which comes ever so close to divine revelation yet misses completely the imperative truth of personal redemption."

With the passing of time, Geoffrey came to be more and more fond of Monica. As yet, however, he did not think of her as the one whom God would choose to be his mate. For Monica felt a growing commitment to return to India as a missionary. She and Geoffrey occasionally discussed this, but never with any thought of going there together.

Geoffrey Lehmann would never be a missionary!

Unknown to him, however, God was at work. For example, something happened during those years at Oxford which had a profound impression upon the young engineer, and doubtless became a part of thought processes which were to so drastically remotivate his future.

He became a close friend of a young chap, neither a Christian nor from a Christian background, whose family frequently invited Geoffrey to their home. On one occasion, he forgot the little pocket Bible he always carried for daily reading. The mother browsed through the Bible, taking note of several verses Geoffrey had marked, and the next time they were together, told him how pleased she was for her son to have a friend with this kind of aesthetic interests.

Oxford and its demands upon the intellect had sharpened Geoffrey Lehmann's witness, and he spent many hours talking with his friend, answering questions and setting forth *ex animo* the precepts of his faith. As a consequence, his friend became a believer.

Now the coin turned, and Geoffrey was no longer a welcome house guest. The mother, who had appeared so pleased with the religious inclinations of her son's companion, became bitter and resentful. At first, this only served to accentuate the young convert's conviction that Christ, received as Lord and Savior, makes a difference to life as well as to the hereafter.

He and Geoffrey shared many spiritual experiences. Of specific significance was their visit to Britain's famed Keswick Conference, where a missionary from China helped the young convert with some of the lingering problems he had in relationship to the initial stages of the Christian faith.

As a result, the young student felt a call in his own heart to the great land of China, then open wide to the bearers of the Gospel tidings.

"It was one of the great experiences of my life, those days at Keswick," the doctor states, "as I counseled with my friend, and knelt to pray with him. It was thrilling to be helping someone make firm his decision to serve the Lord on the mission field."

Not long afterward, however, the young student told Geoffrey opposition at home had led him to give up any thought of missionary service. With this decision came a general deterioration in all aspects of his Christian experience, and the subsequent years of his life became pockmarked with disillusionment and tragedy.

It was a stinging disappointment to Geoffrey.

He plunged with renewed diligence into his academic pursuits, coming to the very brink of culmination, the D. Phil. degree, as it is known at Oxford. His field, the High Frequency Fatigue of Metals. The future, unlimited!

"I must compliment you," Monica said, during one of their family socializings. "You are doing so well at the university. I do pray the Lord will use your skills for His own best advantages."

Even in statements like this, the craftsmanship of God was upon their lives.

As he was writing his D. Phil. thesis, the young engineer felt the need of a brief holiday. Study and research and the pressure of culminating his academic years in high scholarship had left him weary. He also felt the need for spiritual refreshment. And so, since it was Keswick time again, with thousands of Britons flocking to the hallowed grounds, Geoffrey thought he might wisely join them and find for his mind and heart the needed inspiration to crown his remaining hours at Oxford.

Soon the classroom doors would close, never again to open, and he could launch out upon the bright horizons of his future.

One of the announced speakers at Keswick was a furloughed missionary from India. A man with a burning heart and a gifted tongue. In brilliant verbal frescoes, he painted India as it was. A land of over a quarter of a billion heartaches. A land of darkness and superstition. A land of sickness and death.

"Pray ye the Lord of the harvest!" he challenged the Keswick audience. "Pray for the harvesters! We need teachers! We need evangelists! Pray that God will lift young hearts out of the prison of lethargy and complacent materialism, and set them free to pursue the perfect will of God for their lives out on the waiting harvest field!"

Geoffrey Lehmann listened so intently he all but forgot to draw breath.

Then, annointed of the Holy Spirit for a moment of destiny, the speaker exclaimed, "Pray especially for medical missionaries! India needs hundreds of missionary doctors to stem the tide of disease!"

Medical missionaries! The thought struck

at Geoffrey's heart with shattering impact!
It was like God speaking, commanding him
to the harvest!

Medical missions!

But he had just completed his graduate
work in engineering!

Yet he did not struggle. Quietly but
assuredly, feeling in his heart the unmistakable call of God, the call to India as a medical
missionary, he lifted his heart heavenward
and answered, "Yes."

"Of course, I wondered about all the time
spent in the study of engineering," he told me,
"which was only natural. Yet, really, there
was no struggle in my heart. You see, as a
younger lad, I told God He could have all of
my life. I would do whatever He asked. My
heart had all these years been prepared for
this moment of obedience."

But there was one problem, one anguish
that unsettled his mind.

What about his father? All these many
years, his father had labored to build the
business, ever dreaming of the day when
his son, Geoffrey, would complete his education and begin the process of taking over
responsibility.

14 When the Lehmanns sit at meals in
their home at Herbertpur, they face
each other from opposite ends of an oblong
table. Mealtime, always casual, scintillates
with good converstion, giving the visitor his
best observation of these people apart from
watching them at work.

Directly above the good doctor's head hangs

an exceptionally fine portrait of a most comely young woman. She has delicate features, a countenance indicating more interest in sober contemplation than the pursuit of those domestic and social frills by which women are so frequently caricaturized. At my first viewing of the portrait, I had a feeling of the ethereal, which may well have been the artist's intention. Though the portrait does not have that touch of spring and flowers and chamber music, by which artists at one time so frequently embellished young women in oils, the face is by no means cold. It is a face in which one sees wide capacity for kindness and understanding, available without measure, when drawn out like water from a very deep well.

It is a portrait of Monica Allen Lehmann at the time she became the doctor's young bride as, together, they looked eastward toward India and obedience to the call of God.

The doctor had told me, during the shopping tour through the bazaar in Dehra Dun on the morning of my arrival, that Monica Allen was born in India. Part of the reason for their choice of northern India as a field of service stems from the fact that the town in which she was born bordered a Himalayan lake.

India has a village named after General Jacob, whose lineage progressed through seven generations down to the Allen children, all born in India.

Monica Lehmann's maternal grandfather, Colonel Jacob, was a rural engineer, sent to India by the British government to build dams for hydro-electric supply and flood control. He was both a linguist and a man of God, an ideal combination. He post-dated the Lehmann's interest in literature by translating many hymns, serveral of which appear in the hymnal we used each morning at chapel prayers.

Because he spoke half a dozen languages, including Hindi and Urdu, he came to be known as the man who, wherever he might be in the pursuit of his responsibility to his God, brought people together for a Gospel meeting.

He was a man of faith and works, an example of the latter evidenced during one of India's historic famines when he gathered together some forty orphans, purchased land from the government, then settled these orphans on that land in the care of a Christian couple. A little village resulted which, now in its third generation, stands not only as a unique memorial to the good colonel but, even more important, as a witness to the premise that spiritual initiative in India can produce valid redemption trophies.

"It is so wonderful to go there on Sundays," the doctor told me, "to see these people meeting in their little church with no help except visits we have made from time to time."

As do so many people of the area, the villagers wear Punjabi dress. This gives them the appearance of Muslims, a situation which brought duress and suffering during the Partition.

As an example, one family named Ishmael met a band of marauding Sikhs.

When asked his name, the leader replied, "Ishmael, but we are Christians."

"Christians?" the leader of the Sikhs scoffed. "And your name is Ishmael? You are Muslims!"

"We are Christians," the father insisted.

"We worship and serve *Yesu Masih*." He pointed to his head. "See, I do not wear the Mohammedan topi."

But the Sikhs would not believe him and so they cut the man down in the presence of his wife and children. When the wife refused to come with them, since they had killed her husband and she knew all too well what her fate would be, they slaughtered her and her baby and kidnapped her children.

Henry Allen, Monica Lehmann's father, also came from a Christian family. They had not gone to India in government service, however, but to share the industrial glory of Britain's full-flowered Empire.

Many Christians, caught in the spirit of colonialism, fell prey to compromise. Not so Mrs. Lehmann's father. When the time came for him to be made a partner in the family's India firm, he staunchly refused because the factories were kept in operation on Sunday.

As a consequence, he was not endowed like the others.

Later, when the oldest brother died and the firm was taken over by nationals, Charles Allen, the second brother, returned to England and lost all the money he had made during those prosperous years in India.

Henry, who had carefully invested his limited resources, remained in India. God prospered his convictions and his stewardship. He became a lay preacher, well known throughout Plymouth Brethren meetings in India for his radiant, forthright enunciations of spiritual truth.

Sometime previous to this, in the late 1800s, a group of businessmen became greatly distressed over the condition of Anglo-Indian children, which by then was becoming, as it is now, a kind of separate race in the land, the outgrowth of colonial miscegenation.

These Anglo-Indian children, accepted by neither Europeans nor Indians, often subjected to shocking mistreatment, ran like waifs in the streets. At earliest adolescence, many of the girls became prostitutes. Shopkeepers took special precaution against the light-fingered skills of these juvenile brigands.

Anglo-Indian children had no opportunity for education and received no moral or spiritual teaching of any kind. So these businessmen decided to found a school in beautiful Mussoorie, high in the Himalayas. Mussoorie would not only isolate them from the slum areas of the larger cities, but the crisp mountain air would be conducive to study and good health.

So Wynberg School began with five children in a little ridge bungalow.

Henry Allen took a special interest in this school, and made frequent trips to Mussoorie. It was a familiar sight to see him on the school grounds, talking like a father to the children. They loved him deeply, and sat in rapt attention when he spoke to them as a group at morning and evening prayers and at Lord's day meetings.

At this time, Wynberg was primarily a girl's school, with boys accepted only up to the age of nine.

"We must also provide equal opportunity for boys," Henry Allen was ofttimes heard to say. But he never lived to do anything about his special concern. For, while yet a young man, Henry Allen succumbed to heart disease.

112

Remembering so well her husband's dream, the widow provided funds from his estate to build a large main building, so that boys as well as girls might be looked after through the years of both primary and secondary education. Thus Wynberg, the girl's section, stands on a high rise of the ridge, directly down the winding path from Mussoorie's clocktower landmark. On below, some three hundred feet or more by direct fall, stands Allen. The older children attend classes between the two buildings, and no small part of their physical hardiness stems from frequent climbs and descents between classes.

Obviously, India is no place for a fatherless home, so the family returned to England and, by this shape of events, made possible the meeting of the young man Geoffrey and the young maiden Monica.

It was, at the outset, a spiritual meeting.

For, as previously recorded, the young man Geoffrey and his brother conducted CSSM activities during their holidays at the seaside. Destiny walked in the footprints Geoffrey left on the sand as he strolled along the beach in search of those who might wish to attend the CSSM meetings and, coming upon a mother and her daughters, asked if the girls might wish to attend the meeting.

As they got to know each other better, Monica spoke of her dream for the future, to return to India, the land of her birth, and serve as a missionary, making the souls of men the first interest of her life as had been the case with her father.

This in itself, this commitment to missions, in addition to the fact that the girl was slightly younger than he, kept Geoffrey Lehmann from ever so much as thinking God might have chosen them for each other.

There was, in fact, no thought of emotional ties, other than a deepening friendship, until that moment at Keswick, when the young engineering student, ready to unleash his energy to become part of Britain's industrial might, heard the unmistakable call of God's voice.

India!

At this junction in his life, in a measure he had never before suspected, Geoffrey Lehmann became singularly aware of the majesty of God in the lives of those who commit themselves to him.

First, in the case of his father.

"Because of the fact that, as a boy of sixteen, I had told God He could do whatever He wished to with my life," the doctor told me, "my call to India did not come as any kind of upheaval or conflict. It did seem strange that God would permit me to spend all those years preparing to be an engineer, only to have this abruptly changed, but it was in God's hands and I had peace in my heart."

Unrest came as he thought of telling his father.

What would he say to the man who had dreamed these many years of the day when his son, Geoffrey, would take from his tiring shoulders the growing responsibility of the business?

A profound tenderness comes to the doctor's voice, whenever he relates what happened.

"My father was wonderful. He never once mentioned disappointment. He never said a word about problems my decision might bring to the business. Instead, he cautioned me to be sure of the Lord's will, and told me I could pay him no greater honor than to give my life as a missionary. I only hope, if my son ever disrupts my own plans, I can be half as gracious."

The second evidence of the inevitability of God, in the affairs of those who commit their lives to Him, began slowly to dawn upon Geoffrey's mind, as he thought back to that afternoon on the beach and remembered how this girl, slightly younger than himself, had, almost without his noticing it, blossomed into comely womanhood, and as he recalled the many times he had talked with her about the deepest quest of her heart, the quest for India.

He plunged with consuming dedication into the academic requirements of beginning again. But he also began to take sizeable strides toward the winning of the heart of Monica Allen.

She had turned down two proposals of marriage, so intent was her dedication to India, and yet in spite of Geoffrey's change of commitment, and the friendship which had matured between them, she maintained a continued attitude of reserve as their times together increased in frequency.

Like any young woman, Monica Allen was looking for a husband. But, far transcending this human emotion, she was looking for the will of God in every detail of her life.

Normally, it should have taken four years for Geoffrey to complete his medical studies. One week after matriculation, the ruling was changed which had made possible completion in three years.

The Allens lived some one hundred and thirty-five miles distance from the medical campus, and Geoffrey purchased a high speed car to facilitate frequent visits. He gave careful attention to school work, coming off with academic honors in medicine as he had in engineering, but this did not deter him in his rising interest toward Monica.

"You know," he chuckled, "it's a strange thing. Before the Lord called me to India, several young men had expressed interest in Monica. Looking back now, I remember that I was often quite put out at this. Since we were like brother and sister to each other, she shared many of her experiences. I especially remember her asking me about each of the two young men who had proposed marriage. Quite emphatically, although they were fine young gentlemen, I had advised her against acceptance, never once admitting to myself, and surely not to her, any possessive spirit in my own heart."

Now, as the two spent more and more time together, as they talked of the India dream, romance came as a natural result.

"I was so different from her. Full of pranks and enthusiasm, while she was quiet and calculating, but the more I got to know her, the more her deep inner beauty enhanced her outward charm. She was not at all the type of girl I would have imagined myself marrying, and yet the more I knew her, the more I realized that, even if I had never committed myself to India, I could not have chosen a better mate."

It was one those beautiful romances, where the man does not suddenly sweep the woman off her feet with a dramatic proposal but, instead, from mutual understanding and respect, romance grows like the stem and the leaf and the bud and the blossom.

116

Thus came the sublime interlude when Geoffrey Lehmann proposed to Monica Allen.

"We had gone from London to Bath in my racing car, and stopped at Reading for a visit with my sister who lived there. After lunch, as we got underway again, I proposed. I often tease Monica about this, saying I really didn't propose at all, that what I really had done was ask her if she was quite warm enough."

Monica heard what he said, unmistakably.

Her reply, "Yes, of course I will, Geoffrey."

15 Destination India.
Together.

But there could yet be no talk of sailing dates, either upon the seven seas or the sea of matrimony, until Geoffrey concluded his medical studies. Monica, too, needed further training to prepare herself for hospital and missionary service.

In his long discussions with Monica, and his conversations with missionaries from India, Geoffrey realized he needed two special aspects of medical training. He must study tropical medicines. He must specialize in ophthalmology.

In New York, he interned at Manhattan Eye and Ear Hospital, studying with Dr. Castroveyo, one of the world's ablest eye surgeons, some of whose techniques he still uses. For corneal grafting, he practiced at a hospital in Boston. Yesterday's engineer, looking to the size and strength of man's prowess, became today's master of the small and fragile and wonderful human eye.

At last the time came to set a date for the marriage.

While an engineering student, Geoffrey had met a fine old barrister, who had retired from the bench and was living at Oxford. Students came to his house each Sunday afternoon for testimony meetings, remaining to take tea with the saintly man.

"Someday, I would like for you to perform my marriage ceremony," Geoffrey had told him. Plymouth Brethern do not retain salaried clergymen as do other Protestant groups.

By now, however, the man had gone blind, and had committed to memory a marriage procedure of his own which omitted one particular item both Geoffrey and Monica thought must be included. So they had him perform the ceremony, pausing at one juncture for them to insert their own material.

"I remember some of my cousins coming up to me afterward," the doctor relates, "saying they weren't sure we were legally married because the old barrister didn't have a license. I assured them, however, that we had arranged for the local Registrar of Marriages to sit in the hall throughout the ceremony, and this made it quite legal."

Mrs. Allen, the new mother-in-law, had a house in Bath at the very top of Lansdown, and she arranged the wedding breakfast under a marquee looking out across the scenic terrain.

"I was terribly nervous," the doctor says. "Even then, I recognized this tendency toward nervousness as being wrong, because it came from being too much concerned as to what others might think of me."

He sat restless throughout the entire breakfast. To his credit, however, it was more than any lack of self-confidence which kept him off-poise.

His charming bride, much to her pleasure, discovered the cause of his restlessness, when she nudged him and whispered, "Your food, Geoffrey. You have scarcely touched it."

"All these people," he whispered in reply. "They bother me."

"But they're only relatives, darling."

"That's not what I mean. So few of them have any real knowledge of what it means to trust the Lord. I feel I ought to say something to them. Something about the desire of our hearts to put Christ at the very first of all we do."

"Oh Geoffrey," Monica whispered, touching his hand delicately.

"Pray with me about it. I feel we simply must give them our witness, even though it may seem a bit out of place at a wedding."

"If the Lord leads you to give your witness," Monica told him, "it is always in place."

The opportune moment came, and young Dr. Lehmann stood to face the throng of people, a moment's glance at Monica bringing courage to his heart. Radiant from her eyes came the promise of her prayers, a promise he was to see fulfilled times beyond counting in the years ahead.

"My mother-in-law had provided a beautiful wedding," he told me, "The relatives in attendance were, for the most part, wealthy citizens of this present world. It was one of the thrills of my life to stand before them and bear witness, not only of my faith in Jesus Christ, but of the goodness of God in providing lovely Monica to share with me in the coming years of service in India."

Following their honeymoon in the Cumberland hills, they went to Liverpool where the young doctor did his work in tropical medicine while his bride took a course in dispensing.

"It was like a benediction," he said. "We were both able to do well in our studies, rather than being hindered by our marriage."

In fact, the doctor won an honor medal over some fifty others in the group for tropical medicine.

It was the year 1934, and before its end, time for the voyage abroad.

By normal procedure, the young couple would have arranged an itinerary, going from church to church—or, as the Brethren call it, from meeting to meeting—presenting their cause.

"Perhaps it was a mistake that we did not do this," the doctor says, "so we could have had, as do others, a large group of Christians who knew of our cause and could thus remember us in prayer."

While missionary candidates do go from place to place in search of intercessors, realism predicates that this intercession include monetary involvement, and since Dr. and Mrs. Lehmann had arrangements whereby they could provide their own financial needs, they did not feel it necessary to prolong departure. They were young and eager, and the dream of India had burned so very long in their hearts.

"My father provided me with a substantial amount of investment capital," the doctor, who rarely discusses his economic situation with others, told me. "We were actually criticized by some people, who said we were not going out by faith at all. In actuality, though, ours was a very real venture of faith. With my father's counsel, I invested my capital, knowing we would need to live out of the income.

"Many times those first years in India, as the weight of the work grew hard, we realized the lack of intercessors. Many times, too, we could have met the needs more effectively had there been at least a few Christians sharing their tithes. We did not need any money for our own personal support but, especially in medical missions, the potential for helping people is without limits, though it does require funds to do so."

The voyage, by way of Suez, made possible a stopover in what was then Palestine. This experience pulsated with meaning, as they visited place after place made memorable by the life of Christ and the ministry of His disciples.

They strolled though the colorful streets of Jerusalem's old city. They renewed their dedication, to each other and to God, as they stood at the Damascus gate and looked up at Golgotha, to this day giving striking reason for its name, *the place of the skull*. Then, just a short walk further, the Garden Tomb, believed by so many to fulfill the description of *the place where the Lord lay*.

And then back on board ship again, on through the canal to the Red Sea with a stop at Aden before the long waterway to India.

16 India!
At last!

To the young bride, it was home. To the

husband at her side, a way of life totally new and unnerving in its strangeness. But, to both of them, without question, the land God had appointed to be their spiritual inheritance.

After a few days in Bombay, India's most outstanding and most western city, they boarded a train for the interior, on east and north to the Himalayas.

Here they arranged for a pundit, an Indian teacher, to help them with language study. Under normal circumstances, young recruits would have gone to an established language school, but due to their special circumstances, they had neither instructions nor special guidance in such matters, and so took it upon themselves to study privately.

The poor fellow spoke faltering English at best, lacked in a basic comprehension of the mechanics of his own language, and knew virtually nothing of teaching methods. It was not without some difficulty that the young couple communicated to him their desire to dispense with his services.

A hospital at Kachhwa needed a temporary furlough replacement, an opportunity for practical experience while, at the same time, they continued language studies. So, arranging for coolies to carry their few earthly possessions, they set out on foot down the path to the railhead.

It was the time of the monsoons, and the trail was wet from frequent downpours.

"Be careful! Not too fast!" Monica called out in a faltering attempt to communicate her wishes for the coolies to be careful. To her husband, she added, "Do try to make sure. I wouldn't want to have something dropped in all this mud."

"Don't worry, dear." the young doctor assured her. "They are like working men anywhere. They want to do their job well so we will pay them properly."

It all sounded convincing until they came to a swollen stream, the water rushing from a small cascade down the mountain side.

"Shall I carry you, dear?"

"I can walk. But do make sure the coolies are careful with our things."

The young doctor did his best, and the coolies seemed to understand. Carefully, testing each step, they ventured out into the swirling waters. Behind them came the two young missionaries, soon wading to their hips in the muddy current.

"Be careful!" Monica called out.

To no avail, as the coolie bearing their box of clothes on his head slipped and momentarily disappeared beneath the surface, the box of clothing floating freely now with the current.

"My clothes, Geoffrey! Get them!"

But the coolie was back up in a moment. He quickly retrieved the box.

"So sorry, Sahib," he mumbled, looking plaintively at the doctor.

"Don't worry," Geoffrey told him.

Monica could say nothing. She could only watch as the man lifted the box again to his head, and water, saturated with red mountain clay, oozed out from the inside. Tears stung at her eyes, and when they reached the other side, she motioned for the coolie to put down the box.

"Please open it," she said to her husband. "Let's see how badly the things have been damaged."

"It will be quite difficult to open," her husband told her, "and there isn't a thing we can do. We will have everything washed as soon as we reach Kachhwa!"

She stood a moment, looking at the ill-fated box.

"We are missionaries," the young doctor whispered, putting his arm gently about her waist.

She looked at him a moment. A smile etched away the tenseness on her face. A light twinkle brightened her eyes.

"Let's go," she said. "We must not be late for our train."

They walked quietly for several moments.

Then Monica said, "Is it quite some distance from the rail station in Kachhwa to the BCMS Hospital?"

"I'm not sure. But it doesn't matter. We sent them a telegram a few days ago."

"I do hope the wire was received."

"Wire service is quite good here in India. It's their main source of immediate communication. You've told me so yourself. Don't worry. Someone will be at the train station, I'm sure."

The weeks up in the mountains had been a trysting time. A touch of India was there, of course, but the beauty of the mountains temporarily offset in the hearts of the two young recruits the inevitable sense of hurt a conscientious Westerner feels toward the people of India. But the trip by train, across the over-populated countryside, and through village after village after village, reawakened in their hearts the meaning of their mission.

So many people.

So much need.

So little with which to help.

It was at times like this when doubt can rise in a man's heart, and the good doctor does not deny that doubts came to him. What could he do, he and his wife, to even begin to touch a need so great?

As the train moved slowly across the countryside, they talked of the years ahead.

"Have you any further thoughts where we will settle," Monica asked, "after our year at the hospital in Kachhwa?"

"It is something we must study very carefully," the young doctor answered.

Eighty percent of India's population lives in villages, as they both well knew, whereas most missionary work took place in the cities. One might have thought it a natural outcome for these two people, each accustomed to the finest of Britain's living standards, to select one of India's cities. Here they would find progress, the constant trend toward Western ways, in contrast to India's villages slumbering on in the torpor of antiquity.

"Will we live in one of these villages?" Monica asked, turning back momentarily from the train window.

"Perhaps."

"But where? And how will we know to select one above another?"

"The Lord will show us."

They both looked out the window now at the endless stretch of plains reaching out away from the mountains. Village after village. As in the days of feudal Europe, Indian farmers live in villages, for protection and because of their natural gregarious spirit.

Darkness fell, and the train labored on.

"I had hoped we would arrive by daylight," Monica said.

125

They rode quietly for a long while. The villages became tiny clusters of light, here a candle, there an oil lamp, occasionally a cooking fire igniting a larger circle of darkness. It was not beautiful. It was too much a symbol of the greater darkness, with so little light to pierce it.

The doctor put back his head. His bride moved closer, resting her cheek against his strong shoulder. For a moment they slept.

Only a moment.

The train came to a chattering, jolting halt.

"Kachhwa!" a voice cried out.

They struggled to their feet, startled by the suddenness of arrival.

"Remember all our things, Geoffrey!"

"I will. Here, boy," he called to a coolie, "help us with the luggage."

Before the luggage was half off the train, a shrill blast from the engineer announced the departure.

"Geoffrey!" Monica cried out. "The train is leaving, and we don't have all our luggage!"

"Boy!" the doctor shouted, running alongside the moving transport. "Pull the emergency cord! Pull it!"

In another agonizing moment, they got the train stopped, their luggage off and counted. The train moved on, leaving them alone in the darkness.

"Is there no one to meet us?" Monica asked. It was the first either had looked to see.

There was no one.

"Is the train on time?" Monica asked.

"I believe so."

Just then the stationmaster came to them. "I'm so sorry," he said in understandable English, "but perhaps you could help me. I presume you are on your way to the mission hospital."

"Yes, we are," the young doctor said, "and I wonder if—"

"Splendid! Then would you be so kind to deliver this telegram?"

"We would be happy to," Geoffrey said, "but some of the people from the hospital will be here to meet us very shortly, and then you can give it directly to them."

"Splendid!" the stationmaster exuded. "That's a very fine idea. I'll do that." He turned to go, hesitated a moment. "It will be quite soon?"

"We trust so."

"I want to close the station. There won't be another train until early morning."

He stuffed the telegram envelope back into his pocket, and returned to the station.

"Bakshish, Sahib?"

The coolies who had taken the luggage from the train stood pleadingly at the doctor's side. He had forgotten their tip, and took a few annas from his pocket, counted out and gave to each equally.

They counted the coins, a larger gratuity than what they normally received. They looked up at the doctor simultaneously, as though wondering if they should ask for more.

The doctor waved his hand in polite negation, and the coolies walked on.

"Strange no one has come to meet us, Geoffrey."

"They've only been delayed. They'll be here."

But fifteen minutes passed. Then half an hour.

And no one came.

"I don't quite understand it," the young doctor said. "Again and again in our correspondence, Dr. Smith said if we would let him know, he'd be at the station."

"And you notified him three days ago. You said we would arrive Thursday, didn't you?"

The doctor nodded. "Let's sit down over there by the station," he said. "I'm sure he'll be here."

Seeing they had decided to make a move, coolies quickly surrounded the young couple, clamoring for an opportunity to move their baggage.

"*Nahee*," the doctor said, hoping they understood his gestures if not his smattering Hindustani. Then he escorted his wife to a bench near the station, their belongings well within protective sight.

An hour passed. They took a short stroll around the station platform. They peered into the darkness. They came back and sat.

"You stay here, Monica. I'll see if I can get any information inside."

"Your host has not arrived?" the stationmaster asked, as he entered.

"No, he hasn't."

"How very unfortunate for you. It is Dr. Smith who would meet you?"

"I presume so."

A look of dismay came to the man's face. "It is too foolish of me." Once again, he drew the telegram from his pocket. "Dr. Smith was here at this hour yesterday."

"Was he expecting us?"

"I cannot say."

"Perhaps—"

"But how very foolish of me not to have given him the telegram then. It arrived the previous day, on Tuesday."

"Perhaps I should take the telegram now," the doctor said, "so we don't forget to give it to him when he arrives."

"Splendid suggestion. Splendid!"

Dr. Lehmann took the telegram, slipped it into his pocket.

"You say Dr. Smith met this same train yesterday?"

"That is precisely true," the stationmaster replied. "He came on an elephant so he could carry his visitor's luggage." He looked up at the clock. "Oh, but I'm afraid I must close the station securely now. It is already past time."

The doctor returned to his wife, and the two of them watched dejectedly as the stationmaster came out and affixed the lock.

"We can't just stay here in the darkness, Geoffrey."

"Of course not, dear."

The stationmaster came to them. "What shall you do?" he asked.

"That's exactly the question I was about to ask," the doctor said.

"You might hire a *tonga*."

The *tonga* is a two-wheeled vehicle, for hire, drawn by a single horse.

"Could you instruct the driver to take us to the hospital?"

"Most gladly," the stationmaster said.

Fortunately, a man sprawled sleeping in his *tonga* off to one side of the station. He awakened quickly at the sound of the stationmaster's call, and drove alongside the stranded couple and their luggage.

Moments later, they were off through the darkness.

It was ten o'clock when, at last, they had

plodded the two miles from the station to the hospital and, after some inquiry, guided the *tonga* driver to Dr. Smith's door.

"I had so hoped you would send a wire," the doctor said, after he had expressed his great joy at the arrival of the recruits. "I did meet the train last evening, in case you might have been on it."

"I sent you a telegram three days ago, and . . ." Impulsively, if rather slowly, Dr. Lehmann reached for the envelope in his pocket. He handed it to the host doctor.

They could laugh now, for humor and tragedy are such close kin, as they all took turns reading the wire and quoting its contents.

ARRIVING THURSDAY EVENING
GEOFFREY AND MONICA LEHMANN

17 Tea and crumpets and a thousand more words of welcome, and then the host took them to their square, flat-roofed bungalow, half a mile through the jungle from the hospital.

Exhausted, they slept.

But one cannot sleep late, when destiny has newly bared its face. Or, for that matter, when one's bungalow stands no more than twenty yards off from a meandering mud road on which foot traffic and bullock carts move noisily into the dawn, while burden bearing pachyderms trumpet their displeasure at a day begun so early.

The arrivals arose and went forth to behold.

"Oh Geoffrey!" Monica exclaimed. "It's all so lovely!"

The doctor slipped his arm about his

wife's waist. It was official now. They were missionaries!

What a good feeling, to be so sure of the Lord's ordination for their lives. How could he ever have settled for less? And he wondered, at this sublime moment and many times thereafter, suppose the call to India had been spurned, or suppose it had never come? Could he have found, so sure in his heart, this inner peace, this sense of meaning?

They walked to the hospital.

"How very nice," Monica said.

And it was an inspiration for the visual touches they would one day add to their own place.

The buildings formed a square, with a double row on the east and the west, and a large pond in the center.

Very quickly, the newcomers fell into established routines. Breakfast at 6:45, arrive at the hospital at 7:30, major operations until 10:00, outpatients and more operations until 11:30, ward rounds until 2:00, and then lunch.

Rest and study and hospital emergencies in the afternoon, ward rounds again from 5:00 to 6:30, language study with their pundit from 7:30 to 8:30, then dinner and retirement.

The young doctor took to hinterland hospital life with great zest, but not, however, without a few necessary adjustments.

So long as surgery and dressing were kept sterile, he could philosophize himself into an acceptance of greatly lowered standards of hospital procedure. It was a bit difficult, however, acclimating himself to the Indian custom of a patient bringing his family with him. A helpful circumstance, in assisting with minor details and to provide food, but no small problem when, for example, one of them barges into surgery during an operation. Then, too, ward rounds involve a hazard factor when kinfolk curl up on the floor, sometimes as many as half a dozen or more, around the convalescent bed.

"I've got to watch myself all the time," the doctor told his wife, "so I don't stumble or step on someone."

The days at Kachhwa anti-dated modern recovery techniques. Patients were kept prone during hospitalization. Yet some of the most critically ill would get out of bed and move about the ward, scurrying to their cots like frightened mice at first word of the doctor's appearance.

In one of his earliest communiqués to friends at home, the doctor wrote, "Outpatient work is priceless. We have pretty well memorized enough Hindi words, so we can ask questions relative to each prevalent disease, but understanding the answer is quite another matter. We thought one old soul wanted us to give her new eyelashes, until we were able to determine she was going blind because of an eyelash growing back into her eye.

"Work ranges from major operations, abdominal as well as eyes, plus a few tooth extractions. Quite often a patient has been bitten. Bites range from snakes to camels, including dogs, turtles, fish, and, believe it or not, humans. We even do a bit of veterinary work, so you can see our life is both varied and interesting."

One night, as they sat at dinner following the hour's session with their pundit, the doctor asked, "Will I ever master this language problem?"

"Dr. Smith thinks you are doing quite well," his wife reassured. "So do I."

"I suppose I'm so close to the problem, I can't see enough progress to be encouraged. For expediency, I'm finding it necessary to develop my own system of combining limited vocabulary with profuse gestures, which works well enough in medical examinations, but may be a hindrance later on to my proper learning of the language."

"It's the opportunity for ministry that concerns me, Geoffrey. We can witness by life, I know, but I do so long to talk fluently with these people about the Savior."

"In actuality, perhaps, this should be taken care of by our national workers. I can't understand why so few of them are keen about their faith."

"They seem to be interested in the English Bible class on Sunday," Mrs. Lehmann commented. "But the old life continues. I wonder why. Are we a hindrance to them? Is it a lack of prayer concern on the part of people back home? I feel part of the answer is in the spiritual darkness that grips this country. We are in the very midst of Satan's domain."

"What you are saying, Monica darling, is that the lack of enthusiasm on the part of our national Christians indicates an area of potential problem for ourselves."

A look of fear came to the young woman's eyes. "God forbid it! That we should come to India, with our hearts burning to reveal Christ to these wonderful people, and then allow ourselves to grow cold."

"It has happened to others," the doctor said.

They ate quietly for several moments. Then

Mrs. Lehmann said, "It's been six months since we arrived at the hospital."

"I know. I took a bit of inventory just this afternoon. I've done fifty major operations, thirty eye surgeries, including twenty cataracts, in addition to the many other times I have assisted."

They talked on, about the hospital and its vivid demonstration of their dream, the dream of medical missions as a door of mercy to the hearts of lost men. And they spoke of what they had learned about the people. Wonderful, these people. Childlike in joys and deceits, quick to laugh, easily made sad, deceitful and yet wonderfully loyal.

They were a mystical people. Sin at its grossest forms prevailed in their midst. Almost devoid of initiative and perseverance, yet endued with animal-like patience in the face of suffering and drudgery. Loving money, but not willing to work for it. Always quarreling, hospitable, often thoughtful to the needy and the old.

The doctor and his wife spoke more of the problem of converts. Hard by the hospital lay a cluster of huts, built for occupancy by Christians, some of them staff members at the hospital, some of them converted through the hospital's ministry, all needing spiritual nurture lest they fall.

"I wonder," the doctor mused, "I wonder how different, in God's sight, the weak, unproductive Christian in India is as compared to a similar Christian back home."

"I suspect there is very little difference."

"But the weak Christian in England has a church to nurture him. He lives in what is at least called a Christian country. He has temptation, of course, but nothing to compare with the Satanic oppression surrounding these people. In fact, I should think the Christian back home is far more responsible for his conduct than is a Christian in this country."

Yet, even as they spoke of spiritual weakness, they remembered examples of great spiritual strength.

A boy from the northwest who, after carefully considering the Gospel, opened his heart to the Savior. Infuriated, his family made plans to kill him, not only to satiate their humiliation and anger, but as a witness of faithfulness to the way of the Hindu.

A plot was laid to destroy the new convert as he slept.

His sister, though not a believer, loved her brother enough to want him spared. She brought food and a rope to his room, and helped him escape into the night.

After a few weeks, the boy returned to his village, a burning compulsion deep in his heart to proclaim his witness.

"Be quiet," the father commanded.

The Hindi language abounds in polite superlatives, and there is a verb for every mood. The boy chose the forms of most extreme politeness, as he tried to explain to his father that he could not keep silent.

And he did not.

The villagers took him and bound him. As had been done to others, they forced hot oil down his throat as they mocked and cried out, "We will not take your life! We will only take your voice! So you can never again speak of the Jesus religion! Neither will you be able to pray for forgiveness to our gods when you come back to your senses!"

The boy nearly died, and for many months, he could not speak. Earnestly, he prayed for healing. God answered his prayer. His throat healed, his voice returned, and once more he walked the streets of his village, giving witness to his faith.

So his own father had him arrested and put into prison.

Another lad, in similar circumstances, returned to his village, and with what little knowledge he had of the scriptures, preached to his people. The cross and the power of the empty tomb had so captivated his mind he repeated the redemption story over and over.

"Talk about God, if you wish," his people said, "but we do not want to hear about the crucifixion."

"Without the crucifixion," the young man said, "there could be no forgiveness for your sins. *Christ died for our sins.* It is recorded in the Bible. And the proof is in my heart."

"Talk no more of it," they said.

"But I must!"

"If you do, there will be consequences!"

Furious, at the message and at the young man's unwillingness to comply with their demands, they improvised a cross and crucified him. Like the soldiers, they sat and watched him.

All night he hung upon his cross. In the morning, he appeared to be dead.

But a friend, moved by the courage of this young man, took down his body for burial. Then, discovering life, he hid the lad and nurtured him.

"How long will it be," Mrs. Lehmann asked, "until we are permitted to see such faith as a result of our labors?"

"Perhaps never, dear."

"Never?" Tears came lightly to her eyes.

"We did not come to India to win converts. We came to represent the Lord Jesus Christ, to be His instruments. Whatever is accomplished in the hearts of these people must be the work of the Holy Spirit, not simply the fruit of our efforts."

"Is it wrong to want to see converts?"

"It is not wrong, Monica, but it must not be our first objective. We are here at our Lord's command . . . some plant, some water, some gather the harvest. It may be our responsibility to plant and to water, but to never see the harvest."

"Will there ever be a harvest? A great harvest?"

"I don't know."

"Suppose there is, Geoffrey."

"Yes?"

"Suppose there is a great harvest, after our lifetime. Suppose many are converted."

"That would be wonderful."

"Yes, but what of those we shall contact during our years here in India? Must they be lost?"

The doctor did not answer. In these first months at the hospital, full face with India's inexhaustible needs, doubts and discouragements had frequented his thoughts.

Doubts came now to his thoughts.

He turned to his wife, an untouched portion of dinner grown cold on her plate. She struggled against tears, and he stood and came over to her. He put his arm upon her shoulders and stooped to kiss her. She was so often his reservoir of strength. Now she needed him.

They were far from home, the commonplace

comforts and pleasantries but a remembrance. If she could step to a window, and catch a momentary glimpse of England. Passing automobiles on a clean street. Little girls in freshly laundered pinafores. Rows of residential windows, sparkling clean in the morning sun. Pleasingly plump matrons chatting across the washday line.

But there was none of this.

There was only India, and its perpetual need. Wherever she looked. Whenever she listened.

India.

And into this India she would soon bring forth their first-born.

18 They had planned to spend a year at Kachhwa, but remained eighteen months, the time hastened by the growing demands of work to be done, by the deepening sense of their identity to each other, and by those carefree moments, snatched from so many waiting tasks, to share their lives with little Priscilla Ruth.

The added months also gave time for thought, to evaluate the ministry and to discover and substantiate concepts relevent to their call. Increasingly, they saw medical missions as a means to an end.

What end?

Not evangelization.

Not education.

But that God should be glorified!

"When we begin on our own," Dr. Lehmann told his wife, "I believe God wants us to develop a small hospital, with an adequate staff to run it, so everyone will only do half-time hospital work, leaving the rest of the time free for evangelism."

Carefully, they listed the need for personnel.

A lady doctor for the woman's work
A nurse supervisor
Two Indian nurses—one male, one female
A male dispenser
A national preacher
A Bible woman to minister in the wards

"If evangelism is your main purpose," someone in England had asked, "then why go to the expense of a hospital at all? Why not devote all of your time to village outreach?"

In a 1935 newsletter, the doctor replied. "Because it is vital for villagers to get to know us, as they often have weird ideas of why we are doing the work. Such as, for example, stories that we are seeking a baby with white blood, so we can kill the baby because there is a prophecy that a baby with white blood will grow up to rule India. Because the government was building a new bridge near a leper colony here in India and the patients stopped coming to the hospital, believing their bones would be used for the foundation.

"By means of a hospital, we can get a few people from each village to live with us, urged there by their need for medical attention. A week or so of steady teaching on our side, with the opportunity for them to watch Christianity in action, and then they go back to their villages, perhaps not won yet, but good village contacts for us when we want to come in and present the Gospel."

The Lehmanns felt a growing burden in

their hearts for the poor people of the land. In the past, missionary work had been aimed at the high castes, thinking that if the Brahmins were won to Christ, the lower classes would inevitably follow.

Such did not prove to be the case, for in all areas of life, those of the lower castes did not expect the privileges of the higher castes. Many thus came to think of Christianity as a special privilege for the Brahmins alone.

Those missions who had reversed the procedure, giving emphasis to the poor, found that thinking Brahmins, witnessing transformation in the lives of outcastes, sought the Christian faith for themselves.

Kachhwa had also been a proving ground for learning what to do with new converts.

Efforts had been made to bring them into the compound, away from the dangers of village life, so they could be under continual Christian influence. Too often, however, converts, given opportunities for earning money through the auspices of a mission organization, often looked down in scorn upon their poorer village relatives. Then, too, some had professed conversion so that, as "rice" Christians, they could gain a better lot for themselves.

The Anglican Church had followed in the wake of colonialism, ministering to the spiritual lives of Englishmen abroad but also bearing the torch of missionary advance. Good had resulted, but there had also been mistakes. Mistakes like the establishment of so-called Christian villages, where those allegedly converted to Christianity could live apart from heathen influence.

These villages, many of which yet exist in

India, became eye sores to the evangelical cause, sometimes best described by the Apostle Paul's delineation of human depravity in the first chapter of Romans.

No, great though the peril might be, new converts must return to their villages. Many would fall in the face of persecution. Some would lose their lives. But a strong church must consist of believers woven back into the living fabric of the land.

The missionary dare not place a cheap price tag on the Christian faith.

Eager to use Christian literature, the Lehmanns thought to make available without charge all they could possibly acquire and find time to distribute.

People gladly received anything free, they learned, but placed little value to anything obtained without cost. On a trip to one village, they found shopkeepers using as wrapping paper literature distributed free on the missionaries' previous visit. When reprimanded, the shopkeeper asked how it could be wrong, since they had paid nothing for the paper.

In the sale of literature, even at the most nominal cost, only those genuinely interested were willing to pay for such reading material.

The situation was somewhat different at the hospital. Even with charges kept exceedingly nominal, patients often complained at having to pay. With no comprehension of cost, some accused the Europeans of coming to India so they could exploit their poverty.

In extreme cases, when hospital authorities felt sure of man's economic inability, free treatment was given. Only in the most extreme cases, however, since persons who would not

141

pay for their medicine might throw it away unused, questioning its value.

Of course, many of the patients, appreciating the help of the doctors and realizing something of the overbalanced ratio of their cost to service received, paid willingly. But the hospital staff kept constant watch for those who, though able to pay, sought every possible ruse to avoid doing so.

Indian women love their jewelry, often a sign of the husband's wealth, and a woman rarely appears in public without substantial adornment, if she has the means to do so. Yet some women, who could well afford to pay for medical services, traveled long distances to the hospital without jewelry, and dressed in their poorest clothes, so they could avoid obligation.

On one occasion, a government clerk brought his family to Kachhwa. They arrived in a hired automobile.

After Dr. Lehmann completed the examination, and told the man the cost of medicine would be one and one-half rupees (about thirty-five cents), the man threw a tantrum.

"I'm a poor man!" he exploded. "How could you charge so much?"

"But all this does is cover the cost of the medicine." Dr. Lehmann told him. Then, looking out the window, he said, "If you are so poor, why did you come in a hired car? A bus would have been many times cheaper."

Grumbling, the man threw the amount on the table, turned and stalked away.

"Situations like this troubled me greatly," the doctor said. "From the very beginning of our days in India, the Lord answered my prayers in one wonderful aspect. He helped me to see these people, not as a mass but as individuals, and each individual as an eternal soul I might be able to reach with the challenge of the Gospel. So when, for the good of the people, it became necessary to impose restrictions which sometimes angered them, I was greatly disturbed. All I could do was determine to try more diligently than ever to depend upon the guidance of the Holy Spirit for my words and my actions."

The young couple spent long hours together, planning for the hospital they hoped one day soon to build. The doctor carefully checked prices on building materials, the cost of labor. He made many proposed sketches of the hospital, the ground plan as well as the possible façade.

"Shall we put the main entrance here and the operating theatre at this end?" he would ask Monica. "Or should we plan for just the reverse?"

"A great deal will depend on the location."

The place they did not know. But one night, his mind too active for sleep, the doctor thought of how the design might be. In a sudden burst of inspiration, the plan came to him. Vivid and detailed, embodying the many features he and his wife had discussed.

He arose quietly, and set to work on the blueprints. He drew the lines quickly, surely, like a schoolboy tracing a drawing through translucent paper.

Past midnight, when he had finished, soft footsteps drew his attention away from the improvised drawing table.

"Whatever are you doing at this hour, Geoffrey!"

He stood and pointed to the table.

"Monica, there is our future hospital!"

"Really?"

"It came like a flash. I'm sure the Lord gave it to me."

Looking at the drawings, she said, "This is the plan as you envision it?"

"Almost to the square inch, my dear."

"You could begin building tomorrow?"

"First thing in the morning!" He took her hand, held it warmly. "Point to any place on the drawing and I will give you detailed information."

"It wasn't a mistake, was it?" she asked pensively.

"What wasn't a mistake?"

"Your previous education."

"Engineering?" He looked down at the blueprint. "I think we shall see, when the time actually comes to build the hospital, that my engineering background will be indispensable."

He had thought of this before, but it came to his heart again now with renewed warmth. Event by event, God had unfolded the details of his life, each like a pre-cut bit of mosaic filling out the total picture of his life and ministry.

"Have you any thoughts at all of where we will begin our work once we leave Kachhwa?" Mrs. Lehmann asked.

He lifted a corner of the drawing. "The God who gave us our plan will also give us the place," he said. "As we have so often said, we should build on the plains at the foot of the hills."

"But if we find our ministry is to be primarily among hill people, why not build a hospital up among the hills? The heat is so dreadful on the plains in the summer."

"But snowfall can be very bothersome in the winter. This and the cold would make the work difficult. Here's the way I see it, Monica. If we build down on the plains, at the very foot of the hills, the villagers could come down to us in the wintertime. They are accustomed to traveling in the snow. Then, in the summer, we can go up to them with our program of evangelism."

She appeared satisfied with this, but said, "It would be good if we knew the place."

"God knows, and our not knowing may be the very discipline we need to be sure we continue our dependence upon His direction for everything."

The young doctor depended upon divine direction in all of their affairs. But he also believed God despises indolence and rewards initiative. So, as they laid plans for leaving Kachhwa to spend three months at language study in Mussoorie, he began making plans to visit a number of potential areas on the vast spread of plains bordering the great Himalayas.

He did not know by what circumstances, by what unusual circumstances, God would reveal the place of His own choosing.

19 Baby Priscilla Ruth, toddling across the floor to the desk where her father had just looked up from his language assignment, suddenly lost her balance and tumbled. Neither provoked nor discouraged, she got to her feet and tried again, only to fall once more.

So like us, he told himself, *with such a lot to learn before we are ready to serve*. This bit of whimsy became the theme of a letter to friends at home, urging continued prayer for the firm grip of God's hand upon all they did.

When at last the child gave up trying to walk and resorted to all fours, her mother appeared, swept the little one into her arms, and walked over to the desk.

"I meant to show you this map Monica," the doctor said. "It's that map we brought from England."

"The railroad map?"

He nodded.

They had spent hours pouring over it together, trying to visualize the dream of India, as they traced the water courses and the mountain ranges and the boundry lines of this great land.

"Mussoorie is right here in the mountains," he said, pointing. "Just below is Dehra Dun. We could settle there, I suppose, but I feel the need for being a bit more interior, closer to the places where the hill people come down."

His wife leaned down for a closer look.

"See this place here, Monica?"

"Herbertpur." She spoke the name slowly. "Sounds almost English, doesn't it?"

"There must be hundreds of villages in this area, and since this is the only place the railroad people listed, it may be a town every bit as prominent as Dehra Dun. And it's much more satisfactorily situated."

"Is it served by the railroad?"

"No," the doctor replied. He studied the map thoughtfully. "Well, no doubt it is smaller than Dehra Dun, a good deal smaller, perhaps, but I would still presume it to be quite a significant trade center, with a good deal of traffic down from and up into the mountains."

"Herbertpur." Monica repeated. "How far away is it, would you say?"

"From here in Mussoorie? Let's see." He made some finger measurements. "It's fifteen miles down the mountain to Dehra Dun. I should judge another twenty-five miles . . . no more than that . . . to Herbertpur."

The doctor stood, touched his wife's arm with one hand, and with the other caressed the baby.

"For some reason, I feel good about Herbertpur. It seems so ideally situated. Why don't we go have a look?"

So they did.

It was the time of the monsoon, necessitating the greatest of care as they made the four thousand foot descent from Mussoorie to the plains.

In Dehra Dun, they stopped at a shop to ask directions.

"Herbertpur?" the shopkeeper asked.

"It's west of here some twenty-five miles," the doctor said. "I would judge it to be a city something like Dehra Dun."

"The size of Dehra Dun?" the man asked. "Might you be speaking of Choharpur?"

"No, Herbertpur."

"Just a moment," he said, going to the back of his shop. In a moment he returned.

"My associate knows of the place," he said. "Go to the main square, directly at the head of the bazaar, and then turn right."

"That's the road to Herbertpur?"

"It will take you in the proper direction. You may need to ask for more explicit instructions after you have gone a few villages."

The doctor returned to the car, and they proceeded on their way.

"What a strange fellow, that shopkeeper," he said to his wife. "Not even familiar with the cities of this area."

"Perhaps he is new," she said.

It had been a trying journey, the descent from Mussoorie. It was a tortuous journey, the twenty-five more miles to Herbertpur. Rain had left the roads mud-sodden. Farmers, unaccustomed to motorized vehicles, reluctantly gave right-of-way. And the Lehmann vehicle had to ford eight river beds.

Then, at last, Herbertpur.

They might not have found it at all, and could easily have driven through it and on again, without realizing where they were. It was a mere wisp of a place, a tiny bazaar of some ten shops, a few houses.

Then why had it been on the map?

"Our spirits were somewhat deflated at first," the doctor says, "but the more we studied the situation, the more convinced we became that God had, in His wise providence, seen to it Herbertpur was placed on that map of India!"

They could have searched the length and breadth of those plains, without ever finding a place so appropriate. A road from the north, some forty miles long, led down from what in those days were the native states separating India and Tibet. To the west, the river Jamuna flowed out from the mighty mountains on the border of the untouched north, a dividing line between them and the old states of Sirmur and Rampur. To the south, the nearest Christian work lay forty miles away, a distance made even more remote by the Siwalik mountain range, a jetting, jagged ridge, like the irregular teeth of the woodman's saw, standing as if in a valiant but vain attempt to match the mighty Himalayas. Twenty-five miles to the east, the direction from which they had come, was the nearest railhead, Dehra Dun.

In addition to its excellent mountain access, Herbertpur stood at the center of a well-populated, fertile farming area. The doctor drew a circle with a radius only five miles from the center of Herbertpur, and in that circle lay a hundred villages, one of them being Choharpur which the man in Dehra Dun had mentioned.

Thirty years previous, two Europeans had established large estates in the area, one of them a tea plantation. On the tea plantation stood two managerial houses, now no longer needed by Europeans, so let out for rent. At first look, it appeared either of these would serve the purpose perfectly. Neither, however, was available.

Through this contact, however, they found a large empty house, inconvenient in that it stood a mile off the road, but ideal in other important aspects. One wing, attached at the corner by a veranda, could be used as a temporary dispensary, storeroom and operating theatre. Other rooms could be used for recovery wards.

And the rental price was just three pounds per month, less than ten dollars!

November. The year 1935. The Lehmanns took occupancy, and the dream that was India began at last to become the reality which was to become Herbertpur Mission Hospital.

During the eighteen months at Kachhwa, they had carefully followed the scriptural injuction of *"counting the cost,"* budgeting returns from their small private investments so that by this time they had a few instruments, and could lay initial drugs in stock.

Like nervous children unwrapping a gift package, they opened their supplies in the room chosen to be used for consultation.

"I'm terribly nervous," Mrs. Lehmann said. "Afraid we might have done the wrong thing coming here?"

She shook her head thoughtfully. "I can't help wondering, though, if we'll have any patients. Not a soul knows us. How do you propose getting word out that we are here?"

"It may take time," the doctor said.

Any concern either of them may have had as to the availability of patients was short-lived, however. Long before they had finished unpacking, a plaintive cry came from just off the veranda.

"Sahib! Sahib! Daktar Limon Sahib! Kahan rahte hain?"

"What is he saying," the doctor asked, going to the window for a look.

"Your language studies, dear," his wife teased. "He wants to know where Dr. Lehmann lives.

Together, they hurried to the door. It was a great moment. The arrival of their first patient.

From that moment on, patients kept coming. Early each morning, the Lehmanns would be awakened by the squealing of the wheels of bullock carts, as the ill and the infirm made their way up through the tea bushes at the front of the house.

Some were brave, trusting. Others eyed the doctor and his wife cautiously, and no doubt many a bottle of precious medicine in those early days was poured, unused, on the ground, lest the strange man bring harm upon the user.

Patients came so rapidly, in fact, some had to be turned away, told to return at the beginning of December. They came by tens, by twenties, and on Christmas Eve, one hundred patients received treatment.

By mid-January, the daily toll reached as high as two hundred, a number almost impossible to manage.

"What are we going to do, Geoffrey?" Mrs. Lehmann asked late one evening, as they found a moment to pause for breath.

"I've been giving that a lot of thought. I think we have to limit ourselves to eighty people a day, and try to include, as much as possible, only those who really need help. I can't decide if some of these people have only come out of curiosity, or if it is just that I can't manage the language well enough to determine what seems to be wrong with them."

"Language," the young mother sighed. "Between all the work with patients, and looking after Priscilla, I haven't opened a language book for weeks."

"Nor have I, dear."

"At Kachhwa, I had moments of free time when I could memorize vocabulary, even at work, but there is just no time anymore."

"I know," the doctor admitted painfully.

"If this keeps up, we will find ourselves

victims of the very wrong we have set out to make right."

"What is that, Monica?"

"The purpose of medical missions. Our dream was to spend half time in the hospital, half time out in evangelism. But we are busy day and night, seven days a week, just looking after patients."

It was a perplexing time, needing much thought and prayer. The doctor did not know the answers. Nor was he without figments of doubt as to whether or not they had done the right thing, whether God had really led them here after all.

But never, never so much as once, did he lose hold of the abiding peace in his heart, and with this peace came the deep down assurance that God *had* led them. Problems were merely the human proddings a man needs to heighten his trust and solidify his commitment and keep him frequently upon his knees.

They tried to hold the daily patient limit to eighty. More often, the number exceeded one hundred since neither of them had the heart to turn away those who had come some thirty to as much as seventy miles on foot, seeking help.

Throughout December and January, they toiled alone. Only the two of them, day after day. They tried to pace themselves. And perhaps they could have, were their only responsibility that of diagnosis and therapy.

Somedays, however, it took a good share of their time disciplining the patients. There was no one to determine who had come first. They had no receptionist. If a patient grew tired of waiting, he might begin shouting out demands for attention, confusing the doctor so he could not properly carry on his work.

Sometimes patients would mill into the consultation room, even into surgery, but little by little, the Lehmanns succeeded in spreading the word that discipline was to the patient's best interest.

Even so, though apparently meaning to abide by the doctor's wishes, people would congregate in such masses at the door, awaiting their turn for admittance, that the door would give way and three or four come tumbling into the room.

Ofttimes at night, too weary to sleep, the doctor tossed on his bed in search of an answer.

In the face of needs so great, why was there no help?

Why did so few care?

He could think of multitudes of competent Christians back home who, if they would, could find here in India the deep personal satisfaction of knowing their best efforts served the ultimate productivity.

Just one man to help them keep the patients in line. One woman to help with injections and to bind up wounds.

Was it that no one cared? Or had they done wrong in not making better known the dream that had burned in their hearts? Had it been pride, a desire for personal satisfaction, which had led them to come to India backed solely by their own funds?

God knew his heart, how desperately he wanted to be a good steward, to reject the promise of comfort and material opportunity which would have been theirs in abundance had they remained in England. But, in his zeal

153

to do right, might he have done wrong?

Was anyone . . . other than perhaps their closest friends and relatives . . . was anyone praying for them?

It was at times like these that the quiet whispers of promise came again and again to his heart.

They that wait upon the Lord shall renew their strength . . . Lo, I am with you always . . . Call upon me, and I will answer . . . Your heavenly Father knows what things you have need of.

In the midst of turmoil, uncertainty, he rested upon the unfailing promises!

Early one morning, as they prepared for the day's routines, a stranger came to the improvised hospital. Mrs. Lehmann took him first to be a patient.

"I am in quite good health, praise the Lord," he said, in fully understandable English.

It was startling, this kind of conversation after weeks and weeks of nothing but the chatter of Hindu patients.

"Geoffrey," Mrs. Lehmann called softly, as she excused herself and slipped for a moment into the hospital, "we have a visitor. He seems to be a Christian."

The doctor came quickly.

"I am an Indian evangelist," the man said, after the three had introduced themselves. "I heard of your work, and felt the Lord's call to see if I might be of assistance. I could remain for perhaps two or three month's time."

Surely God had heard their cry for help, and this was His answer!

They engaged the man on the spot.

He immediately solved the problem of making sure patients received attention in the order of their arrival, a need of long standing, but more important, he devoted much time each day to preaching in the courtyard and to individual counsel.

Busy as they were, the Lehmanns could not resist an occasional moment at the window those first days, their eyes moist in gratitude as they watched the evangelist at work and listened to the silver flow of his tongue.

Soon after the arrival of the evangelist, a dispenser, well trained at an American hospital, offered his services. In addition to being an able pharmacist, he could give anesthesia.

The India dream had never been more real!

In March, a permanent evangelist arrived. A good educational background had not spoiled him, and he served the hospital well as a man of zeal and intercession and practical knowledge.

At the end of April, the doctor and his wife tabulated the patients who had come to the hospital.

January	1,478
February	2,000
March	2,040
April	2,404

In January, they sold 121 Gospels, 226 in February, 266 in March and 839 in April. With each Gospel, they gave away a free booklet defining the way of salvation.

Mail was scarce, and many times undependable, but they were able to keep in contact with folks at home.

The doctor's father wrote to inform them he was spending much time in prayer, seeking the Lord's will as to the continuing part he should play in the India dream. He would stand by them with additional finances as the work grew.

Thus the ministry flourished and the fame of Herbertpur spread across the Jamuna lowlands and high up into the hills. Little-by-little, they grasped the language. With the help of their evangelist, they planned weekly treks out to the villages, holding Gospel services. At first they spoke by interpretation, then gradually on their own. It was good to see how the rapport of the hospital opened the way.

One morning, when the houseboy returned with the mail from Herbertpur, he brought a letter from Mrs. Lehmann's mother.

"I am so longing to see you," she wrote, "and to meet my grandchild, Priscilla Ruth, I have booked passage on a steamer bound for India."

20 The visit of Monica's mother, Mrs. Allen, brought multiple blessings. She was a woman of charm and affection, and she once again touched their lives with those domestic graces they had so often taken for granted at home.

She adored her new grandchild, giving her hours of attention, and thus relieving the doctor's wife for better service to the hospital.

Mrs. Allen had spent most of her early life in India, so they called upon her frequently to assist in the question and answer phases of diagnosis. Her help brought to at least temporary termination an accumulating series of laughable anecdotes.

The doctor had understood one man to say his sister had been badly hurt in the jungle, blood and milk issuing from her torn chest.

The man was instructed to keep the woman warm and comfortable, and to bring her to the hospital as soon as possible. At dawn, the man appeared with a nanny goat so badly hurt she was unable to feed the little kids born two days previously.

Another man waited his turn in line and, when he came to the consultation room, said he himself was not ill, but had brought someone who was. There were an unusually large number of patients that day, and several had pushed their way into the examination room, clamoring for a moment of the doctor's attention. Above the din, the doctor tried to get more information, finally concluding the man had brought his brother.

"Bring him in," the doctor said, "and I will see what is wrong."

"Dr. Sahib," the man said politely, "he is too big to come through the door."

The doctor looked at the door in unbelief.

"If you could just give me some medicine to cure his fever, I could give it to him, and he will not need to come in at all."

The doctor and his wife tried without success to persuade the man to bring his ailing brother into the consultation room. At last, though contrary to their principles of good practice, they made up a prescription. The man took it gratefully and left.

"Too big to come through the door?" the doctor said to his wife. "Whatever can he have meant?"

Then, all of a sudden, it hit him. The man hadn't used the word *bhai* (pronounced bah-ee) for "brother" at all but, instead, a similar word *guy* (pronounced gah-ee) meaning "cow."

"It is one thing to give wrong medicine,

because of our inadequacy with the language," Mrs. Lehmann told her mother. "But what if someone wants to know the way to Christ, and we use the wrong words in giving instructions?"

All too quickly, Mrs. Allen's visit passed, and she returned once more to England. The doctor not only loved his mother-in-law, but got along with her handsomely. So he missed her. But as welcome as her visit had been, the help she gave at the hospital caused an even greater sense of loss.

If only he had more time for concerted language study.

By no means did the Lehmanns assume a careless attitude toward language, even though the pressure of responsibility gave so little time. Whenever they could snatch moments to do so, they worked on grammar and vocabulary. But the ablest schoolmaster of all turned out to be the people themselves, the simple, conversant folk chattering about their aches and pains and, with the growth of their confidence in the doctor and his wife, about their families and their way of life.

More and more, the Lehmanns ventured into the villages, proclaiming by witness and through literature the verities of their faith.

Did the people understand them? Was there a flicker of comprehension, when they spoke of sin and God's judgment and the provision of cleansing through the Savior's blood? Or did the people listen only out of courtesy, as an expression of their gratitude for what the doctor and his wife had done for them?

One afternoon, a woman came to Mrs. Lehmann, and said, "The first time you visited our village, we did not understand what you told us. The second time you came, we understood a little bit. Now this third time, it is much clearer to us."

The Lehmanns took courage, and stepped up their efforts.

India is a land of religious festivals, sometimes observed by a *mela*, or fair, held in each village or at some central place. People come in throngs to a *mela*, and the doctor and his wife were quick to see the opportunity for spoken witness and the sale of literature.

With the aid of their evangelist, and a continuingly more effective grip upon the language themselves, they increased their effort to use the hospital itself as a means of witness. The doctor began to offer phrases of spiritual counsel to patients during consultation and treatment. They secured a "magic lantern," a slide projector illuminated by a gasoline wick, and gave Bible lectures each Sunday night in the garden. Villagers thronged to the showings. One Sunday night, when the lecture was finished and the lantern put away, a large group arrived from another village, so the doctor repeated the evening presentation.

During all this time, the Lehmanns prayed for converts. They fully understood their place in the harvest, the necessity of faithfulness and complete dependence upon the Holy Spirit for fruit, and yet they longed to see visible evidence of the Gospel's power.

Such evidence came one night, at the close of a lantern lecture, when two people came and, kneeling in the presence of their friends and relatives, openly professed their desire to bare their hearts to Christ and turn from their sins.

During the eighteen months at Kachhwa, the doctor and his wife had learned to temper the vivaciousness of their own faith, and the constant desire to see immediate growth in a convert's life, with the grim realities surrounding the work of God among people so deeply steeped in ignorance and spiritual darkness.

Even so, their hearts ached as, one by one, people who professed conversion gave no subsequent evidence of spiritual growth.

It was true of many.

But there were lasting results, good sheaves in the harvest, and though they numbered but a few, they became enriching trophies of the grace of God.

As confidence grew in the hospital and in the integrity of those who ran it, the Lehmanns found warm welcome whenever they took time to visit a village. They made a special point to visit the homes of new converts, and again and again saw evidence of the fact that their expressions of friendship enhanced the possibility of a convert's living at peace in the village.

With growth came the need for more facilities.

"We can do only a small amount of surgical work, due to the limited space at our disposal," the doctor wrote in one of his letters to Britain. "There is a small shed near the house, which we use for eye and medical and surgical wards, and the hospital itself can have as many as fifty patients and their relatives congregated in one night. Our dispensary is well fitted now, but much too small. It is difficult to use the stethoscope, when people ten feet away clamor for medicines. We must soon begin building, and yet we dare not until we have additional helpers!"

More and more of the hill people came down for attention, a glow to the hearts of the doctor and his wife, for the people of the hills had been central to the India dream. Some days as many as fifty came. One morning, an old man staggered into the compound bearing his wife in a basket on his shoulder, confident of the doctor's ability to make her well.

Back in England, the doctor and his father had talked of establishing a mobile unit with which to bring medicine, and the Gospel, into the hills. But foot journeys into the highlands revealed an almost complete absence of roads navigable for automobiles, so the doctor abandoned the idea.

His father and mother came to India for a holiday visit, while the doctor and his wife yet operated the hospital in rented quarters, and immediately the elder Lehmann wanted to know about plans for ministry in the hills.

"A mobile unit simply isn't practical," the doctor said.

"But wouldn't you reach more people, Geoffrey, if you could get closer to them?"

"No doubt of that, Father."

"Then why not establish a hill station? You and Monica could get away during the hot months, and still continue your work."

There was one motor road up into the Himalayas from Herbertpur, and it led to a picturesque village called Chakrata. At first sight, the doctor's father fell in love with the place, and promptly initiated plans for the purchase of a house suitable for use as a dispensary.

The Lehmanns used the Chakrata station

effectively for several years, until demands on their time at Herbertpur made continuance impractical. They pleaded and prayed for sufficient staff to fill this potential-laden ministry opportunity, but none came.

Medical work would remain geographically central to the India dream, but first and always must be the spiritual objectives, glorifying God in the daily display of their lives, reaching out to lost men and women through literature and the proclamation of the Gospel.

One evening, some months later, as they strolled in their little garden, the doctor and his wife discussed one of the growing concerns upon their hearts, the longed-for day when congregations could be established in the villages.

Hand-in-hand they strolled. A warm sense of oneness entwining their hearts.

"Those two letters from London," the doctor said, "the one from my father and the one from the chap who handles our investments."

"Yes?"

"I'm amazed at the way God's provision continues to keep pace with the growth of our work."

"You shouldn't be amazed, Geoffrey. It's all part of God's promise to us."

"I know. But I have had my moments of questioning, our manner of support being so different from the normal case with missionaries, and wondering how many people we really do have praying for us."

He paused to prune the dead limbs on a small bush growing off to one side.

"To have a strong church," the doctor continued, "people must at least be able to read the Bible."

"They need schools," his wife said.

"Exactly! I think we should give careful consideration to establishing some schools in the area."

"Geoffrey! With all the work we have now!"

"But there are Christian teachers available, and we would only need to be sure we had schoolmasters able to take care of administrative details as well as teaching. Just this afternoon, as I took a moment to watch the evangelist in the hospital courtyard, and saw how intently so many of the people listen to his message, I couldn't help praying for the day when we will have congregations of Christians here in India, just as we have back home."

"The evangelist is doing an excellent job, isn't he?"

"I'm very pleased," the doctor said.

They turned now to return to the house and, as they did, saw one of the staff members approaching in considerable haste. Anxiety was written full across his face. He glanced about in the hope no one saw him.

"Is something wrong?" the doctor asked.

"Oh Dr. Lehmann!" the staff member began, struggling to sustain composure, "the evangelist has just been found in the act of deep moral sin!"

21 The fall of the evangelist was a stinging disappointment, driving the Lehmanns to a deepening realization of their need for intercession.

The evangelist confessed in tears, and received the doctor's full forgiveness, but he had soiled his witness among the people, and could no longer continue at the hospital.

Dr. Lehmann wrote to the missionary who had sent him, expressing concern lest any failure on their part had caused the man to fall, and received a reply stating the man had been sent away from his previous place for a like offense, but the Lehmanns had not been advised in order to give the fullest opportunity of a second chance.

"The Lord used this experience to teach us an important lesson," the doctor believes. "We must not have paid evangelists. The evangelist should be like us, a worker at the hospital who gives his witness out of the abundance of his heart and not for the purpose of monetary payment. Through the years, as we have followed this policy, we have seen the wisdom of it. Patients respect the witness of a man whom they have seen at work at the hospital, along with the doctors, looking after their physical needs."

By 1937, work began on the Lehmanns' home, the new hospital and worker's quarters. It was an exciting venture, not only the fulfillment of so large a part of the India dream, but opportunity for the erstwhile engineer to employ some of his latent skills.

They progressed slowly, having carefully budgeted each stage of the project against their known supply of income. It took until 1940 to complete the initial stage of the building program, consisting of an outpatient department, a laboratory, a small surgical theatre.

They were now seeing three thousand outpatients a month, in addition to surgery. The fame of the hospital spread in an ever-widening circumference.

One man expressed his gratitude by letter:

Dear Sir,

The medicine you send wife has done no harm, so please send more. Think she suffers from dystepisa or some other disease. Her liquoice is now much better.

A man came into the hill dispensary, and commented on a picture of Jesus which Mrs. Lehmann had hung on the wall, in which Jesus was shown healing a blind man. The hill man's wife had told her husband the story of how Jesus healed with a single touch. Another woman from the same village had brought a dying child to the dispensary, and the story spread that the child had been completely healed after one dose of medicine.

So when Mrs. Lehmann gave the hill man his prescription, and told him to come back for more when it was gone, he said, "Why should I come back? I shall be all well."

Expression of trust in the doctor did not always assure proper adherence of directions on the part of the patients, however.

One old woman, given medicine to take back to her village, appeared a few days later, when the doctor and his wife were in her village selling literature and giving their witness.

She came to Mrs. Lehmann and said, "I am a poor old thing, I just don't understand all you were saying, but I am listening."

As the two talked further, it seemed the woman had some misgivings about the way she had been treated at the hospital. The doctor's wife pressed her further, and learned the old woman had been told to take her medicine for three days. Thinking how much better it would be to regain her health in one day, she took all of the medicine at once, and became distressingly ill as a result.

Another woman who came to the dispenser's window one morning, was given fluid medicine and told to shake the bottle vigorously before each dosage.

"The bottle? Shake the bottle?"

"That's right," the dispenser told her.

The woman mumbled something about her husband not being able to read too well, and so he must have misunderstood previous instructions when he vigorously shook her each of the three times she had been instructed to take medicine.

The work was growing, the dream coming into reality, but not without the doctor drawing upon the full composite of his business skills to make ends meet. They would build well but they would also build efficiently. They must not go into debt. So the doctor shopped everywhere for best prices. For while the home and the hospital must be built, out of their own supply of funds, they must also keep the ministry going at full outreach.

"We both became so weary," the doctor told me, "we felt we had to take a short furlough. The Lord sent a relief doctor to help us, a person of fine training, skill, and dedication, and so we felt we could slip back to England."

In a London display room, the doctor's fancy was caught by a fine automobile. They could use it on furlough, then bring it back with them to India.

"I bought the car," he said, "but later felt I had done wrong. We could much better use the money to build a ward included on the hospital blueprints."

His father offered to buy the car. Then, when their sailing date came, he gave them the car plus a substantial gift sufficient to construct a new ward.

As adroit stewardship made possible the building program and an enlarging ministry, additional workers came to help staff the hospital. Among them, Dr. Zingers, who worked hard hand-in-hand with Dr. Lehmann, then shouldered the fullest share of the load during the initial months of World War II when the doctor left the hospital to join the Indian Medical Service, a part of the British armed forces.

Meanwhile, considerable effort was made to establish schools, where children could learn the basic three Rs.

They established the first school at Dharamwalla, a little forest village some five miles from Herbertpur, with children coming from half a dozen other villages. The enrollment quickly grew to over sixty children.

When Hindu schoolmasters expressed animosity to the idea, and went to several of the villages stating their willingness to open schools which, they promised, would greatly exceed in benefits those sponsored by the doctor, the villagers said, "When no one cared for us, the Sahib cared. He gave us medicine and offered to teach our children. Why is it you now are so suddenly interested in us?"

In one village, the weekday school gave birth to a Sunday School, and the Lehmanns hopefully thought this might develop into the first of the congregations they envisioned through the villages.

At Mehuwala, a village four miles from the hospital, the villagers themselves came to the doctor, urging his help in starting a school.

"Not only must our children learn to read, Doctor Sahib," the villagers said, "but we, too, want to learn."

Adults did attend the school, including an old man of seventy, searching his way out of the abyss of illiteracy alongside his eight-year-old granddaughter.

Opposition continued, as fanatic religionists appealed to government authorities to close down the schools, but the educational program prospered, so much so that the Lehmanns came to think of the schools as offering more spiritual potential than did the medical work.

Chief agitators were the *Arya Samajists*, an iconoclast movement of reformed Hindus determined to rid India of Christianity and its influences, and to uphold the Hindu religion as the only religion of the land. The *Arya Samajists* unleashed the fury of their opposition at both the hospital and the schools. Because of the great reservoir of good will already established as a result of the Herbertpur medical ministry, and realizing a man does not value education as much as he values his health, they majored their efforts on abolishing the Christian schools.

The initial tactic was to build Hindu schools in the same village where the Lehmanns had initiated educational work, warning the people to expect the unleashed anger of the gods if they permitted their children to be influenced by the Christian religion.

Where threat and competitive efforts did not avail, they sometimes resorted to outright physical attack. At one school, the doctor was called to a village where the schoolmaster had been severely beaten.

On another occasion, an older teenage boy attended one of the schools, not only did well with his books, but listened intently to the Bible stories. Sometime later, he married.

One day he came to the schoolmaster, telling of a dream he had had. In the dream, he found himself wandering in a great city, the like of which he had never before imagined, and as he awakened, it came to him that this city must have been the heaven he had so often heard the schoolmaster talking about.

"I should like very much to know more about the way to heaven," he told the schoolmaster.

So, at the pedagogue's invitation, he came regularly for teaching and, after some months, asked to be baptised.

Others from the village expressed growing interest, too, and when members of the hospital staff came for Gospel services, many people came to the school, joined in the singing, listened intently to the preaching.

The doctor and his associates envisioned an entire village turning to Christ.

Time came for the young man to be baptised, and the doctor made preparations for this to be an event which would bear memorable witness to the other villagers.

A little stream was selected near the village, and a time set for the baptismal. An hour before the service, curious villagers began to gather, bringing joy to the doctor's heart, as he and Mrs. Lehmann and members of their staff approached the scene.

The appointed hour came and passed.

The people grew restless and mumbled among themselves.

The baptismal candidate did not appear.

"Do you suppose something could have happened to him?" Mrs. Lehmann asked her husband.

"I don't know."

The doctor now spoke to the people, thanking them for coming but stating the service would be postponed until some other time.

Then he said to his wife, "Move among the people. Some may be interested in literature. I'll see if I can find the young fellow."

He was not to be found. In his fear, he had fled from the village.

It seemed to be a bitter defeat for Christ's cause!

One night, the schoolmaster was awakened by his dog barking. It was the young man again, who now poured out his heart in repentance, saying he felt like Peter, denying his Lord as he had done. He asked if he might live at the hospital compound, to hear further teaching.

Of course, the doctor gladly made arrangements.

Some weeks later, when the grip of hot weather had moved fully across the countryside, the doctor was awakened by frenzied shouting about the compound. He quickly dressed and went out to investigate.

The repentant young convert had been kidnapped.

Dr. Lehmann, inquiring for details, learned that two men had been seen taking the young fellow and leading him off down a nearby trail through the fields.

"How long ago?" the doctor asked excitedly.

"One half-hour's time, Sahib," he was told.

Running full speed, he headed off down the path. His shoes fell off, but he kept going.

"It was early morning," he recalls, "and patients coming in their carts to the hospital must have wondered what had come over me."

Presently, in the distance, he saw the boy being led away by two rather large men.

"Wait!" he called. "What are you doing there?"

The men kept going, but since the young man held back, impeding their progress, the doctor soon reached them, stepped in front of them, and firmly planted his feet in the path.

"I want to know what you are doing," he demanded.

"This man has a small son," one of the abductors said.

"His son is very ill," said the other.

"We have come to take him back to his village, so he can be with his son."

"You shall do no such thing," the doctor said. "I'm sure you are lying, and there is nothing at all wrong with his son."

Onlookers gathered, as is inevitable in Indian country places when something out of the ordinary occurs, and the two men slowly yielded to the doctor's prestige and power of persuasion.

"Let the young man come with me," the doctor said. "I will arrange for one of our workers to go to your village, and see if the child is actually ill. If he is, we will have him brought back so I can look after him myself."

Later that day, a hospital worker dispatched to the village found no evidence whatever of illness on the part of the child, confirming the doctor's suspicion.

Incensed at being affronted and humiliated, the men who had instigated the trouble stepped up their opposition. They demanded the young man be brought to trial before the head man of the village.

"The schoolmaster forced him into saying he is a Christian," the agitators said. "Or perhaps he is being paid to make the claim he has changed his religion!"

The doctor readily agreed for the young man to be brought before the village council.

"Why did you become a Christian?" the head man asked.

"It was not the work of the schoolmaster, but the power of God's Book," the young man said. "This book was like a window into my heart. It showed me my sins, but the book also told me of *Yesu Masih*, who came to die on the cross for my sins. I was not forced in any way, and I was not given any kind of payment. It was the power of God's Book that changed my life."

The people of the village were visibly impressed by the young man's witness. The head man stood and rebuked those who had stirred up trouble. He took the side of the young convert. It was not the schoolmaster at all, nor the people at the hospital, but God's Book which had the power to change lives.

Shining victories in the ministry of the schools, though they brought much encouragement to the Lehmanns, served also to instigate the inevitable rise of continued opposition.

"If we had conducted the schools on a

completely secular nature," the doctor says, "perhaps we would have had no difficulty. But we could no more maintain schools, without using them as a means for Christian testimony, than we could run the hospital without making use of every opportunity to give our witness."

The influence of the schools, together with the continuing ministry of the hospital, gave fruit in conversions. It was a gleaner's harvest at most, with multitudes hearing Christ's message but only an occasional individual proclaiming acceptance. Yet, in the light of the Savior's assessment of the worth of a soul, the doctor and his co-workers rejoiced over each victory, and implored Heaven's guidance on the care of new spiritual babes.

Should they send them away for Bible training? If so, where?

The more they discussed and evaluated, the more convinced they became that young converts should return to their villages.

"Decisions like this are sometimes excruciating," the doctor says. "If we see every professed convert as an individual, eternal soul, and we surely do, then ought we not to exert every possible effort to nurture this convert? This we want to do, most surely, and we have always made every effort we can to encourage young Christians. But, deep in our hearts, we have had the continuing conviction that, important as the individual is, we must build on principles which make a sure foundation for the future."

As a result, there have been converts who have braved the fires of persecution, but there have also been many unable to stand against persecution.

The doctor tells of one young man, eager to identify his life with Jesus Christ, who remained in his village. Opposition raged against him. He could not buy at the shops. He could not grind at the mill. He could not drink at the well.

When his wife and children were taken from him, his courage waned. He came furtively to the hospital, told the doctor he could no longer witness as a Christian.

"In the hope of encouraging him," the doctor says, "we went on occasion to his village. At first he would meet us and talk to us. But, finally, he hid himself whenever we came. He did not go to the heathen ceremonies, but neither did he any longer bear witness as a Christian. I wonder how we would get on if we were just young Christians, not able to read much, having no Christian fellowship. What kind of witness would we maintain in the face of heathen opposition?"

Opposition to the schools continued, like the coils of a constricting serpent, until one by one they had to be closed. Thus came into focus, more clearly than ever, the doctor's understanding of the problems he faced.

The opponents of the Gospel could not silence the hospital, *The Jesus Hospital*, as it came to be known by the people. The hospital stood on ground owned by the foreigners, its rights protected by the constitution of India.

They could, however, set up their defenses and launch their attack in the villages. Christianity must not be allowed to permeate the villages. For Hinduism is more than the religion of these people. It is family and possessions. It is culture and customs. It is the sum of all life.

It is also the past and the future, as taught in the Hindu doctrine of reincarnation.

The Lehmanns saw clearly the stature of their response to the enemy. The spiritual worth of the hospital must be ever strengthened, for without this foundation upon which to continue building the India dream, the future was but a chasm, wide enough and long enough and deep enough to consume the very dream itself.

22 In 1941, Britain stood alone. Hitler's Panzer divisions had stormed across Europe. Belgium and Holland bled at the throat! France groveled in subjection. Pearl Harbor had catapulted the United States into the South Pacific. All earth trembled.

To multitudes of common folk around Herbertpur, however, the war was a thing far removed, and to some a thing unknown. The hospital pulsated with activity, three thousand outpatients a month and all one hundred beds constantly in use.

But newspapers and radio reports told of the need for doctors in the armed forces, and deep in Geoffrey Lehmann's heart stirred the spirit of England. He spent many hours in contemplation and prayer.

"What shall I do, Monica?" he asked his wife, as they walked one evening in the garden.

"You have every reason to stay," she said.

"I know."

"God called us to the hospital, before the war ever started, but on the other hand, if England falls, the cause of missions may also be lost!"

"Then I have no other choice."

He went to the nearest army headquarters, reported the work he was doing. The commanding officer told him they considered the medical contribution of Herbertpur vital, and said they would not ask him to join unless a crucial emergency should arise.

Content, he returned to the hospital.

It was good. Monica was a woman of courage, but he did not like to leave her alone here in India. Her responsibilities had increased with the birth, in March 1937, of their second daughter, winsome little Petronella Anne; Peta, they called her. May 1940 marked the birth of son Donald. And there was always the daily uncertainty of need at the hospital.

A few months later, however, he received a letter. The government needed every available doctor. Would he be willing to enlist? This he did, and wisely so, for shortly afterward virtually every British doctor in India was drafted.

It was to be in some respects a mundane experience, the puerile instances of officers pulling their rank, the day to day routines, and he thought often of the more meaningful warfare against disease and ignorance at Herbertpur. But the army did have a shortage of pathologists, a field of medicine in which he had special training.

So he was able to give worthy service to the crown.

But the weeks dragged into months, then years. Weeks and months and years filled with loneliness for his family and the work at Herbertpur.

It was tolerable at first, with an active staff maintaining the hospital ministry, but one by one members of the staff left, and the dreaded day came when Monica and the nurses shouldered the task alone.

"The Lord gives wisdom and strength for each day," Monica wrote. "We are doing the best we can with His help. We all miss you deeply and pray for you. Prilla and Peta pray for their daddy every night."

Would the war never end, and release him for the tasks to which he had offered his life?

One day, he received a letter which struck panic to his heart. His beloved Monica, suffering from a suspected malignancy needed immediate attention.

It was a case of prayer being answered before he called, as an eminent surgeon had just arrived from England, and agreed to take the case if Monica could come to the military base.

He sent an immediate wire.

It was a tense morning when, as the resident pathologist, it fell the husband's responsibility to prepare sections of the removed growth for laboratory study.

"In our lab," he says, "we diagnosed the growth as benign. To be sure, however, we sent a specimen to Bombay."

The report came back malignant!

At times like this, the width of their shared dedication and the depth of their love for each other shone like the sun. Monica did her best to keep cheerful. She spent hours with her Bible, resting in its promises, firm in her belief that God is God, whatever the circumstances of the moment might be.

Once again divine fortuity intervened. A specialist arrived from England. He examined the section with great care, as the concerned husband looked on with bursting tension.

At last, the specialist turned away.

"It is a very early form" he said, "and has not yet become malignant."

Mrs. Lehmann returned to the hospital. She saw between fifty and sixty outpatients daily, with such effectiveness that on a subsequent occasion, when the doctor returned for a short leave, and his wife asked him to examine an elderly woman, the patient said, "No, I don't want to see you. I want to see the real doctor."

She pointed to Mrs. Lehmann.

With the hospital on a limited schedule, Mrs. Lehmann turned more and more to her cherished interest, village evangelism. On several occasions, during my brief weeks at Herbertpur, I traveled with the Lehmanns to the villages and watched in sheer admiration as these busy people took time for open air witness.

It touched me profoundly to watch Mrs. Lehmann. She was always the first to sing out the lead notes of a song, the others joining in. As she sang, she looked out at the people gathered around, her gaze encompassing them with love and concern.

When the war ended, the army transported the doctor, his wife and family back to England for demobilization.

Dr. Lehmann took additional studies, completing work for the diploma of ophthalmic medicine and surgery.

Meanwhile, back at Herbertpur, a staff member by the name of Mrs. Childs, an old doctor and a spinster nurse, endeavored to keep the work going.

One day, the Lehmanns received word from Mrs. Childs.

The nurse had received a proposal of marriage by mail, but at first said she could not remember the man. His name and face must have come to mind, however, because a few weeks later, she arranged to go to Bombay to marry him. It turned out the young man, who made the proposal, had left the army with the idea of becoming a missionary, but mission leaders in Bombay insisted he be married. He looked through a list of suitable names, until he found the name of the nurse at Herbertpur, whom he somewhat remembered.

With the departure of the nurse, it was impossible to keep the work going. Herbertpur Mission Hospital closed its doors!

The Lehmanns' first impulse was to leave England immediately. But, convinced of the need for further training, including two months at the Eye Bank in New York, the decision was made to delay.

For twelve months, the hospital stood empty and unused.

Would the Arya Samajists move in, intimidating the caretakers and decimate the property? Would the people, with no one to assuage their ills, abandon confidence?

"We bathed the waiting ministry in constant intercession," the doctor says. "Eagerness rose in our hearts such as we had not known since those earlier days before we came out to India."

A year had never passed more slowly. But it did pass, bringing the day of *bon voyage* for India.

On the boat coming back, they first heard of Partition, ominous news accounts of bloodshed and suffering along the border of India and the old Punjab, now Pakistan. The hospital stood near the Punjab, with mingling villages of Hindus and Muslims. Would the soil run red at Herbertpur? In the blindness of fanatic frenzy, might those once loyal to the hospital turn against it and destroy it?

A new urgency to pray gripped the Lehmann family.

Arriving in Bombay, they immediately attempted to make contact with the hospital. There was no response, and for an entire month, they waited. Dispatched telegrams brought no reponse. Due to the tenseness of the situation, no trains ran to the north.

"It was a time of great testing," the doctor remembers. "With the hospital surrounded by both Muslim and Hindu communities, we scarcely dared think what might have happened."

At last they got a train to Mrs. Lehmann's childhood home and, a bit later, passage to Dehra Dun, each of these trains under heavy guard by special army police.

Arriving in Dehra Dun, they quickly arranged transportation to the hospital, tension rising in their hearts as each mile brought them closer.

When they came up the small road leading to the compound, no one could speak. They turned in at the gate. The lawn was kept. Flowers bloomed in the garden. But the house and the hospital stood as inert as a photograph.

As they stopped outside the house, Mrs. Childs, God's faithful appointee during these interim months, heard them and came out.

"Geoffrey! Monica!" she gasped. "The Lord

be praised!"

"How is everything?" the doctor asked, almost afraid to venture the question.

"All is well." Mrs. Childs spoke firmly. "Nothing has been harmed."

"Praise the Lord!"

That very evening, the doctor began a re-study of blueprints for completion of the entire complex, confidence aglow in his heart. The India dream had never been more real!

23 By 1954, the initial blueprints for Herbertpur Mission Hospital could be relegated to the archives. A diesel electric generator provided direct current lighting for the hospital and the houses and alternating current for X-ray. Modern sanitation was also installed.

In a report to his friends, the doctor wrote: "We now have two operating theatres: the first, a modern type general theatre with one of the newest anesthetic machines, special lighting, etc.; the second, a dark theatre for the eye work. The completed hospital contains eye wards, male and female general wards, a midwifery and tuberculosis block, and private rooms for paying patients. We have enlarged the Indian workers quarters, built a nurses house, and enlarged the cottage in which Dr. Peter Warlow and his wife, who have just joined us, now live.

"From time to time new workers have come, and now the Herbertpur group has a strong European as well as an Indian section. Too much could not be written to tell how these have given all they have to build up

the work and reputation of the hospital to
its present level.

"The choice of a position for the hospital
has been amply justified. The hill people turn
to it in their troubles.

"They look upon it as their own hospital,"
said the chairman of the Choharpur town
council, "and will go nowhere else. Throughout the district, Herbertpur has come to be
known as *The Jesus Hospital.*"

The addition of Dr. and Mrs. Warlow gave
new stature to the work. Peter combined skill
in his profession with a radiant love for
people and a commitment to Christ uniquely complementary to Dr. Lehmann's years
of initial ministry. Annette Warlow, Peter's
wife, though these were the years when her
children were young, lifted her share of the
load without hesitation, a trained nurse and
a woman of compassion and heart and soul
of a missionary.

Still one more new face graced the Herbertpur scene in the birth of Susanna Joan, a
December 1946 arrival, named for an aunt
who had died three years earlier.

For a period after the Lehmann's return
from England, the school ministry continued.
Mrs. Childs had been able to acquire a suitable piece of land in Mehuwala. Previous
quarters in Mehuwala had been in the low
caste section of the village, so the high caste
people would not send their children to it.

Five people were baptised at Mehuwala,
and a great crowd gathered for the event,
among them a well-educated, high-class
Hindu whose heart was so deeply touched
by what he called the "beauty of Jesus
being shown," that he went back home and

preached to his family, all of whom were converted.

Another patient from Mehuwala had had a successful cataract removal at the hospital, returned to his village to say that, before the operation, the doctor prayed with him, praying in the same name the schoolmaster used when he prayed.

"When the bandages were finally removed," the man said, "I could see, and I fell at Doctor Sahib's feet to thank him, but he raised me, and lifted my hands toward heaven saying I should thank the One who lives there, for it was in His name and for the love of Him the work had been done."

As a result, the man became a believer.

The Lehmanns' vision of indigenous congregations springing up among the villages had not yet come to reality, however. Among those who heard God's message and professed to believe it, some continued to falter in the face of community pressure and persecution. But, one by one, through the ministry of the hospital and the sale of literature and the open air witness to the villages, men and women turned to the living God.

An old man from the hills had gone to the bazaar to purchase a second-hand coat, in the pocket of which he found a picture of Christ hanging on the cross. The story of Calvary was completely unknown to him, and he looked in great wonder at the picture, showing it to his friends.

No one understood it.

He kept the picture and, sometime later, made his first trip to the hospital, bringing his wife for treatment. There, for the first time, he heard the message of the cross, and immediately identified the words with the picture he had found in the old coat.

He listened in rapt attention, then purchased a Gospel which he took back up into the hills, so he could read for himself, over and over.

A Muslim holy man came for a cataract operation, and made his way to the little chapel for the Sunday afternoon service. He, too, listened in wonder to the message of redemption.

At the close of the service, he came to a member of the hospital staff and said, "I have traveled all over India, seeking to know God's truth, but I have never heard anything like the good news I have heard here."

He was given counsel and instruction, and left the hospital with the avowed determination to bring to others news of the great joy born in his own heart.

On ward rounds one morning, the doctor came across a *Sadhu*, a Hindu holy man admitted during the night, and proceeded to examine him. He would require perhaps a week in the hospital. As he so often does with new patients, the doctor spoke with him about the spiritual purposes of Herbertpur.

"If you please, Doctor," the man interrupted, "I would prefer that you do not talk to me about this. I am a very religious man myself, and I do not need the Christian faith. I have come to the hospital, because I have heard of the good treatment you give, and this is all I want."

Somewhat taken back by this frankness, the doctor managed a cordial exit.

At five o'clock that evening, as is customary in the hospital, staff members conducted evening prayers in the male wards.

"This is fine for the poor, ignorant people who come, and have not had an opportunity to study the great truths of religion," the *Sadhu* mumbled, "but it is of no value to me."

Day after day, though, he listened.

As he regained physical strength, he attended evangelistic services in the courtyard, watched the weekly lantern slide lecture.

Then the day came for his dismissal.

"I'm going to give you this additional medicine to take home with you," the doctor said. "Take it if you have any recurrence of your ailment."

Then the doctor turned to go.

"Please, Dr. Sahib," the *Sadhu* ventured shyly, raising his hand. "I would also like to purchase a New Testament."

Coyly, the doctor said, "A New Testament? But I thought this was the side of our hospital work which did not interest you. You only wanted our medical treatment."

"That was true when I first came," the *Sadhu* explained, "but I have been listening to the words about Jesus, and I have seen the kindness and love shown by the staff, and now I have come to love the Lord Jesus Christ, and I want to have a New Testament, so when I go to the villages of India, I will no longer tell people about the Hindu religion but, instead, I will tell them what the Lord Jesus Christ means to me."

A doctor in Calcutta arranged for his son to enter the Indian Civil Service, and to marry a girl of the family's choice.

"Father," the young man said, "my life is full of confusion. It has no meaning, I seem to be searching for something, but don't know what it is. Please excuse me from marriage, or from taking the position you have arranged, and let me pursue the study of the Hindu religion."

To this his father agreed, and the young man spent several months in initial study, then became a disciple of a renowned holy man, looking after the holy man's needs, preparing his food, learning at his feet.

In time, the young man also became a *Sadhu*, with his own disciples but without the peace of heart for which he so long had sought. He was made one of the priests at a temple near the hospital. One day, when staff members were in the village preaching, he purchased a Bible.

The Bible did not at first bring peace to his heart. Instead, it revealed his problem, his sin, and night after night he went out into the jungle, falling upon his face in anguish of heart.

Then one night, something he had read from the Book flashed through his mind. *Believe on the Lord Jesus Christ and Thou shalt be saved.*

"The words came to my heart like fire from the sky," he later told the doctor, "and I cried out to God in belief. At that moment, I received the peace of sins forgiven for which I had been seeking all my life."

He went from the jungle to Herbertpur, to the hospital reading room, and told the one in charge what had happened. They spent the greater part of the night in prayer and fellowship.

Then came opposition.

The head priest of his temple had him seized and beaten. (An interesting sidelight to this part of the story is that the priest sat drinking a few days later, when another drunk fell upon him and beat him so badly he was carried back to the temple unconscious.)

The young convert continued his witness, until one night fellow priests kidnapped him and took him to a secluded hut, holding him captive for several weeks until he escaped. He came to the hospital, and told Dr. Lehmann his story.

Here was a prized trophy, and the temptation ran strong in the doctor's heart to offer him refuge at the hospital. But the wisdom of the years led him to urge the young convert to go back to the village, though he carefully warned him of possible consequences.

"I will go back," the convert said.

"We shall all pray for you here," the doctor assured.

He returned, like a soldier briefly rested from battle who once more faces the enemy. He was ridiculed. His life was again and again jeopardized. But he maintained his witness.

"The Christian *Sadhu*," the people called him, some in ridicule and some in respect.

Months later, on a return visit to the hospital, he talked with Doctor Lehmann about the possibility of baptism.

"I must make a confession, Dr. Sahib," he said. "I have been poisoned, imprisoned, many times rebuked for my faith, but I somehow cannot summon the courage to be openly baptised."

He walked away from the hospital compound in deep sadness.

When quite some time went by, and he did not return, the Christians at Herbertpur grew worried, and two of the workers decided to look for him. They headed toward the highlands, since people of the area, when they run from danger, often seek a hiding place in the hills.

After considerable searching, and finding no news whatever of the vanished man, the disappointed hospital workers sat for rest and to partake of some food they had brought with them. Should they return to the hospital, or continue their search?

Together, they prayed for guidance.

Then one of them lightly knocked over a little pile of leaves near where they sat, under which was some money. This they took as a sign from God that they should go on.

In the very next village, as they inquired about the Christian *Sadhu*, some hunters said they would find him hiding in a cave up in the hills. The hunters gave detailed directions.

The hospital workers found the fugitive in dire physical straits, and gave him the money discovered under the pile of leaves.

The converted Sadhu came with them to the hospital. He subsequently received baptism, but asked that the baptism be private, not open so his friends could see, which imposed a limitation upon his witness, though he continues to be known as the Christian *Sadhu*.

On another occasion, as the doctor made hospital rounds, a man with an injured knee drew his attention to say, "I believe in *Yesu Masih*."

Skeptical, lest the man have in mind better treatment as a reward for temporary acquiescence, Dr. Lehmann spoke with him cordially, but avoided discussing his claim of conversion.

A few days later, his injury having sufficiently responded to treatment, the man left.

"Suddenly," the doctor relates, "I remembered what he had said to me, and felt deeply ashamed that I had not taken time to speak with him further. We had been especially busy, and the incident served as a rebuke to my own heart, helping me to once more reaffirm to myself the fact that I was a missionary medic, not a medical missionary."

Fortunately, however, while the doctor had been remiss, one of the Indian compounders, sensing the man's interest at afternoon prayers, had conversed with him at considerable length.

The doctor said to the compounder, "Help me try to find this chap. Let's ask patients who come from his area."

Six months slipped by, until one day the compounder came to Dr. Lehmann with the information they had been seeking. It was immediately decided the compounder should make an effort to re-establish contact, and so as soon as he could dispense with his responsibilities at the hospital, he mounted his bicycle and rode away.

It was a trip of forty miles, quite some distance along a river bed over which the compounder had to walk, pushing his bicycle, but at last he reached the village and found the professed convert talking with several people.

At sight of the compounder, the man stood to his feet and exclaimed, "There is the man from the hospital, where I learned to know *Yesu Masih!*"

Though he could not read, and though he had spent only those few days at the hospital, the man had grasped enough of the meaning of Christian faith to give his witness to the entire village. As a result, one prominent village man expressed interest in becoming a believer.

Not only had the new convert witnessed in his own village, but he had gone to weddings and community gatherings elsewhere, asking permission to tell of his new faith.

He came often to Herbertpur for fellowship, and members of the hospital staff, including Dr. and Mrs. Lehmann, went to his village whenever they could to encourage him.

As the years passed, he suffered much persecution, especially from his brothers. They burned his crops. They drove away his cattle. They made him a spectacle in the presence of others.

Undaunted, he went on witnessing.

One day he said to the doctor, "You know, I think of the worm that lives in the dirty earth, and is then changed into a beautiful butterfly. I was just like that. I was like the dirty worm. Now, through trust in *Yesu Masih*, I feel the freedom and joy of a butterfly!"

He was subsequently baptised, and through his witness, his wife, his younger brother, and two nephews were also converted and requested baptism.

His older brother continued opposing him, often resorting to violence.

"I pray continually for my brother," the man told workers at the hospital. "Sometimes, perhaps it is only for a moment, he listens to me. I believe God speaks with strong words to his heart, but Satan snatches the words away."

The man became a special trophy, and members of the hospital staff often spoke of what it would be like if a hundred such men were scattered among the villages around Herbertpur.

One day the older brother committed suicide by throwing himself into a well. To this day there are many, even among the Hindus, who believe the brother did so because of the weight of conviction of his own sins.

Another man, converted at the hospital, went back to his village to bear witness of the transformation in his heart. At first, others in the village limited persecution to scoffing. This in itself is no small torture, when one realizes that for many of these people, what happens in the village and in the immediate area surrounding, adds up to the entire sum of life. Horizons are small to a poverty-ridden Indian farmer.

One day he came to the hospital, and told the Christians he wished to be baptised. Members of the staff began immediately to give him careful counsel.

"It is a constant problem," the doctor states, "knowing when to permit baptism. Whereas it seems in the early church the people were baptised when they believed, I remember our very first convert. We waited some months until it seemed we could not refuse him baptism any longer. Yet, after we had done so, we realized we had acted too quickly. For he had problems of backsliding soon afterward. We feel if we had taught him more, he would have been better able to resist temptation.

Baptism has come to be recognized by heathen and Christian alike as a decisive seal of commitment in India. A man who says he is a

Christian can stay in the village, buy at the shops, drink from the well, be accepted as a member of the community. Not until after baptism is he taken to be a real Christian, and thus subject to total persecution.

"As I have thought of the early Christians," the doctor says, "I have often wondered how they practiced baptism. When we first came to India, we felt baptism should be a witness to everyone. But did the early Christians practice public baptism? More likely the rite was performed in the secret of the catacombs."

So it was that the man in this case received careful counsel, to make sure he knew what he was doing.

"I want to be baptised," he said. "Whatever the cost may be, my heart belongs to *Yesu Masih*. He was nailed to a cross. They beat Him and spit upon Him. He did this for me."

He was baptised.

News spread quickly to his village, and as he returned, several of the men waited for him, blocking his entry on the path.

"You are now a baptised Christian," the village leader said. "You are a fool."

"You no longer belong in our village," said another.

A third man stepped up to spit full into his face.

"My house and my land are legally mine," the Christian said quietly, "and the faith that I have in my heart bids me live at peace with everyone."

The village men lost some of their boldness in the face of the quiet confidence expressed by the Christian. They let him pass on up the road to his house. But not before the headman said, "Your house and your land may be yours, but our ears belong to us and we charge you never to speak the name of *Yesu Masih.*"

But the man could no more forbid witness from his heart than he could deny breath to his lungs. Christ had transformed him, and the evidence shone from his life and flowed from his lips.

One day the men of the village came to his house.

"You have not obeyed us," they told him. "Speak once more the name *Yesu Masih,* and we will hang you over a slow fire and burn your Christianity out of you."

The Christian was frightened, and grew more cautious. Yet he continued to witness.

The threat of burning was not carried out, but his relatives came and took his wife and children away from him and he was denied water at the well and food at the shops.

One day he came to the hospital.

"I can no longer speak the words that are in my heart," he said, his head hanging in contrition. "The courage to witness has gone from me. But I have not given up my love for *Yesu Masih.* It is with me forever."

The doctor looks with infinite tenderness at those who falter in their faith.

"We have no idea of the Satanic pressure these dear ones face," he says. "It is amazing to me that so many have stood the test."

In discussions with missionaries on many fields, but particularly in countries designated as heathen, I have often broached the subject of the lost state of the heathen.

One field leader told me, "The biggest problem we face is with missionaries who don't really believe the heathen are lost. They see the endless masses of people in total spiritual blindness, and try to rationalize that God will somehow spare them from eternal judgement."

Dr. Lehmann has a firm theology on this. To him there is no question of every man's need for individual redemption. But, knowing the country people so well, he understands their capacity for spiritual light.

He says, "I believe we shall meet hundreds in heaven, who died with a simple belief in the Lord Jesus Christ. Maybe all they experienced was the new birth, without sufficient light to have what the Christian usually thinks of as conversion."

I talked with him at length about this, for the subject fascinates me, and was particularly interested in what he had observed of the death of the heathen.

"It's amazing, really, how quietly they die," he said. "Death comes to them sometimes in an agony of pain, but not in an agony of mental distress. I think the mental struggle comes with those who have heard of the Lord and refuse to accept Him as their personal Savior. On their deathbed, they realize what they have done. Those people who have never known the Lord seem to have nothing of that deathbed struggle."

I have thought much of the doctor's words, and have wondered anew at the glory of divine light and the individual responsibility of having fully seen this light!

24 From the very first day, I saw the hospital as something far removed from the production line therapy which so often characterizes medicine in my own country. Each patient who comes to Herbertpur is a personal entity, not a mere name on a file card.

There are file cards, to be sure. In fact, because of the vast numbers of patients who come, daily numbering into the hundreds, Herbertpur Mission Hospital has of necessity become one of the best organized institutions of its kind anywhere.

On arrival, except in cases of emergency which must have immediate attention, each patient receives a chit designating his number. Since so many cannot read, colored lines, painted on the floor, tenacle out from the main diagnosis area to various places the patient may be asked to go.

I have watched an hour at a time, as the doctor consults patients. Each receives a warm greeting, often a friendly touch on the hand or arm. It does not take long until an inept linguist, such as myself, begins to pick up threads of conversation.

"Dard kahan lagta hai!" the doctor asks. It simply means, "Where do you feel the pain?"

"Dard meri pet men hai," the patient may answer, gesturing to his stomach.

The doctor may then emit a sympathetic sound, caused by stacatto contact of his tongue to the back of his teeth, as he says, *"Mujhe afsos hai."* As a friend's good neighbor might respond to the news of illness, the doctor has said, "I'm sorry."

He then writes a prescription or instructs the patient which line to follow for additional tests. Though hundreds of patients may be seen in one given period, this sense of warmth and sympathy and respect for the dignity of each individual is always there.

Peter Warlow in his conduct with patients, Annette Warlow in the many responsibilities she expedites so well, Esther Kunz and Monica Lehmann, wherever I saw these people at work, the philosophy of being "missionary medics" stood out in obvious heartening visualization.

It was as a matter of fact, the continual evidence of this kind of spirit which prompted us to include a brief scene in the film *Tashi from Tibet*, in which the girl Angmo, Tashi's sister, is influenced to become a Christian, after she says, "The love from the Christians, it is everywhere in the hospital."

Strong though the emphasis may be to express love and consideration for each patient, and high and diligent the standards of medical care, nothing in the ministry at Herbertpur supercedes the concern for new converts.

For the church in India is not some kind of religious social club, as is so often the case in America. The church, among these villages, is individual members of Christ's body, as yet unidentified with any temporal organization. They are seedlings for the future. Few in number. For the most part, weak.

While great care is taken not to produce incubator Christians, once members of the hospital staff become convinced of a convert's sincerity, they do all they can to strengthen his cause.

On occasion, the doctor has called on the police, since the constitution of India guarantees religious freedom. The law should actually be on the side of the convert, though the fine letter of the law comes slowly across a land so steeped in tradition.

"Do you see any lessening of persecution?" I asked the doctor, as we talked one day.

"Sometimes it would seem so," he said. "Perhaps if they were left to themselves, with no outside agitation, the villagers who know of our work here at the hospital would accept new converts just as they accept us.

"The number of Christians increased quite rapidly in India until the time of Partition, when the British government evacuated. Since then, we find the numbers beginning to go down. No doubt many thought that, since the British were supposedly Christians, it was an advantage for them to follow suit."

"Would this not tend to upgrade the quality of those who now become Christians?" I asked.

"In a sense, yes. What India needs . . . and this ought to be the subject of our greatest prayer concern . . . is that there may be Christians, even those such as ourselves, who are concerned about being good examples. But it is so difficult these days to find Indian Christians who are really keen about their faith. Even here at the hospital, with such wonderful people on our staff, we so often find the tendency for our national co-workers to become lax in their spiritual lives, and to show no real zeal for the things of the Lord."

"What about those areas where there are established churches?"

The doctor shook his head sadly. "Thank God, there are exceptions," he said, "but for the most part, I fear the Indian church is sadly in need of renewal."

The content of this particular discussion with the doctor lingered long in my thoughts. As a result, my research included a considerable amount of time tracking down the two things he had talked about. Outside influence causing village agitation against converts, and the need for spiritual examples.

The more I thought about it, the more I realized how the ministry of the hospital itself uniquely fulfilled the requirement of providing a good example. True, because of its immense prestige, the hospital's spiritual example depended upon the kind and effectiveness of ministry among those who came for treatment.

But there was also another side.

The doctor and his co-workers, like the young converts sent back to the villages, also faced persecution. And the attitude of reaction to oppression was frequently open to public observance.

Perhaps Dr. Lehmann will never know the covert efforts that have been made to silence the hospital forever, both as a lighthouse of the Gospel as well as a medical center. On more than one occasion, threats have been made, indicative of the likelihood that contrary minds ponder ways to forever silence the ministry.

At times, local medical men have expressed displeasure toward the hospital, jealous because of the vast numbers of patients who come to Herbertpur, animosity because the nominal rates charged do little more than cover the cost of medicine.

One doctor went to the extent of putting a man at the road by the entrance to the hospital. He told all manner of falsehoods about the work, but few paid any attention to him.

Of course, there are many reputable Indian physicians and surgeons who not only respect the doctors at Herbertpur, but count them as their friends. Some of these men refer patients to the hospital. When the occasion to do so arises, the doctors at the hospital refer patients to them.

Patients come to Herbertpur who have been badly treated by village quacks. One particular problem consists of what is called couching, a cataract treatment performed in the village by which the lens of the eye is pushed. This gives the patient immediate vision, but always with the end result of permanently lost vision, usually in one or two years.

These so-called doctors may also use infected needles. All have inadequate medical training. They go from village to village with the prime purpose of making money.

It goes without saying that these quacks, again and again exposed by the men at Herbertpur, lie awake nights pondering ways to decimate the effectiveness of the hospital.

In the forefont of opposition has long been the *Arya Samajists*. They are a reformed group of Hindus, who have ceased from worshipping idols. They emphasize the philosophic aspects of the Hindu religion, and look for the day when intellectual Hinduism shall be the religion of India.

The *Arya Samajists* violently oppose Christianity, and continually exert pressure for all missionaries to be expelled from India. They speak of Christianity as being like a monkey, with the foreign missionaries as its head. Cut off the head and the body will die. They have instigated newspaper accounts of alleged evils perpetrated at the hospital, and have gone so far as to travel from village to village with loud speakers, urging the populace to rise up en masse, and forcibly drive out the foreigners. People were urged to stone the doctor, when he came to their village. Such agitation was not without its measure of response among some villagers. The great reservoir of respect and appreciation for the hospital, however, prevented serious action from materializing.

One day the District Magistrate, chief civil officer of the area, called Dr. Lehmann into his office at Dehra Dun.

"Dr. Lehmann," he said, "I have full authority to close down your hospital, and I have been thinking about this. We appreciate the medical work being done, but you must cease preaching Christianity to the people."

The doctor, who is not beyond bristling when the occasion arises, said, "My good man, I don't know whether you have the authority to close down my hospital or not, but I do know that so long as I am working at Herbertpur, I shall run it in the way it has been run these past years, and we shall continue to preach the Gospel."

"But you are taking advantage of poor, unintelligent people," the magistrate argued. "They do not come to you for your religion. They come for medicine and your skill as a doctor. You should talk with intelligent people like myself."

"I shall be very happy to talk with you about my faith in Christ," the doctor said, "and your need for Jesus Christ. You know, the Bible tells us, *all have sinned and come short of the glory of God.* This is why God sent His Son into the world."

When he could finally recapture his poise,

having been so completely thrown back by the doctor's verbal craft in the situation, the magistrate exclaimed, "No! No! I didn't mean you should preach to me!"

"But a District Magistrate's word is his bond," the doctor said. "Now that you have told me I should preach to such as you, isn't it rather strange you should not want me to do so?"

The end result was that the D.M. became quite friendly, and listened with considerable interest as the doctor presented to him the claims of the cross. Though he did not profess conversion, he and the doctor became good friends.

A group of men, plotting ways to silence the hospital, gathered in one nearby village.

One man sat quietly for awhile, then stood to say, "You don't know what you are talking about. I was ill for several years, and spent a lot of my time trying to get help, but I couldn't find it anywhere. I was about to commit suicide, when someone suggested I go to the Herbertpur Mission Hospital. I did, and they cured me. There I learned to know the Lord Jesus. I often went from ward to ward, playing the gramophone records, so others might hear about the Lord who had done so much for me. You men should go to the hospital and see for yourselves that all these things you say are not true."

The opposition quickly dispersed.

From the earliest days in India, the Lehmanns have recognized the *mela* as an unprecedented evangelism opportunity.

Each *mela*, a Hindu religious festival, draws thousands of celebrants sometimes from a distance in excess of one hundred miles. For most, the *mela* is a time of excitement, but a few sincerely seek religious truth.

Other sheep have I which are not of this fold, Jesus had said. To the Lehmanns, these were the sheep without a shepherd, led astray by superstition and fear, and it was the Christian's solemn duty to tell them of the Savior's intervention on their behalf.

Armed with scripture portions, tracts and books, staff members gave open-air witness. With nothing but carefree thoughts, people gathered in large crowds to listen. Hundreds purchased literature. Many asked questions. Sometimes discussions took on an amiable classroom flavor and lasted for an hour and longer.

"I think we at Herbertpur have come to think of the *mela* with more excitement than the people themselves," the doctor says. "It is such a marvelous opportunity to lift up the Savior."

The *Arya Samajists*, incensed by the effectiveness of missionary ministry at these festivals, heightened their opposition.

At a 1945 *mela*, for example, the Herbertpur folk erected a literature tent, as a place for people to stop and read and as a base for open-air witnessing and literature sales. From the outset, they detected undercurrents of hostility.

One evening, an Indian friend came with word that, after nightfall, a large band of men planned to encircle the tent, setting it on fire and destroying anyone who might be inside. So staff members took down the tent and returned to the hospital, praising God for this obvious evidence of His protection and praying that the seed sown might bring a good harvest.

One year, the undercurrent of talk ran so strong at *mela* time that police officials came to the hospital, and urged Dr. Lehmann to refrain from evangelistic activity at the *mela*.

"Gentlemen," the doctor said, "I'm sure we have proved to you that we want always to comply with your requests. We want to be good, law-abiding residents of this wonderful country. I'm sure we also agree, however, that we have our rights, just as much right under the constitution to present our faith as others have the right, which we readily agree, to oppose our faith."

"But we fear there may be trouble," the police chief said, documenting his statement with numerous reports that had come to his attention.

It was a painful decision to make, but as staff members carefully assessed the situation, it appeared obvious that any effort to evangelize at that year's *mela* would mean certain trouble. This they did not fear, except that opposition's fanaticism currently ran at fever pitch, and bloodshed could easily result, greatly hindering the reputation of the hospital.

Reluctantly, they decided against an appearance that year.

They did make arrangements for putting up a large tent in a nearby city, however, securing the services of a converted Muslim as evangelist, a man of good reputation and with a sizeable knowledge of India's religions.

Not until the tent was erected did the hospital staff realize a nearby house served as special headquarters for the *Arya Samajists*.

In the middle of the first sermon, enemy

forces beamed a large speaker toward the tent, drowning out everything that was said.

"We sent a message to them," the doctor tells, "offering to debate, and they accepted our offer."

The *Arya Samajists* chose a prominent *Sadhu* to confront the evangelist. It was a tense situation, as many people gathered, but a unique spiritual opportunity none-the-less.

After the debate, someone from the crowd called out to the *Sadhu*, asking who had won.

"The evangelist won on nearly every point," the *Sadhu* admitted.

As a result of this statement, he was almost mobbed and, later, as he walked down the street, Hindu boys threw stones at him.

"It was quite an amazing thing," the doctor says, "a Hindu *Sadhu* chosen by the *Arya Samajist* headquarters, to oppose us, being stoned on our behalf!"

One amazing aftermath to the tent meeting debate was the fact that the librarian at the *Arya Samajist* headquarters, so impressed by the logic of the evangelist, asked that two Bibles be placed in their library.

Tension ran high during the remaining services, men coming in to shout defiance during the preaching, but the mayor of the little town intervened with police protection. As a result, the mayor became a close friend of the hospital, and has come to Herbertpur since for special treatment. He and his wife show a real interest in Christianity.

In the following year, the staff once again instituted plans for evangelism at *mela*.

The *Arya Samajists* were waiting for them, surrounding them and following them from the moment they stepped into the *mela* grounds, shouting above the voices of staff members as they gave their witness.

"Americans! Americans!" they taunted. "Beware of these people! They are spies, living off of foreign money!"

"We are not spies," the doctor told them. "Furthermore, we are not Americans. We are from England."

"You lie! You lie!" the fanatics cried out.

Literature sold by hospital personnel was grasped from people's hands and torn to shreds.

"These men actually became so violent," the doctor says, "that we feared for our lives. I remember with gratitude how one young man walked alongside me, telling me he was all against these kind of people, and for us not to think they in any way represented the true spirit of the people of India."

After some three hours, realizing every attempt at witness would be shouted down, and seeing the people were already so intimidated they did not dare to purchase literature, the doctor decided they should return to the hospital.

"We were terribly discouraged," he says, "wondering had we really been in the Lord's will. There were so many things we could have done at the hospital during this time."

The very next morning, however, a young *Sadhu* awaited the doctor, as he emerged from his house.

"May I have a few words with you, Doctor Sahib?" the *Sadhu* asked politely.

"Of course," Dr. Lehmann told him.

"I am the son of a wealthy furniture manufacturer. I was given an opportunity to enter my father's business. But I longed for spiritual peace, and for the last five years, I have searched all over India for this peace. I have been to all the holy places. I have been the disciple of a holy man. I came to the *mela* seeking peace. Then I saw you there. I saw on the faces of you and your people that you could be at complete peace, even when surrounded by such a vicious enemy. In return for unkind words and brutal acts you gave kind words and pleasant smiles. This peace I must find for myself."

He found it.

A short time later, when the doctor was showing lantern slides of *Pilgrim's Progress*, the young man came to him and said, "I was just like Pilgrim. I had a burden of sin and sadness, and now it is all gone because Christ has taken it from me."

So, again and again, God caused the wrath of man to praise Him. As in the case of Job, however, a man may face all manner of external problems without a waivering faith. The real test comes when God permits bodily affliction.

Shortly after the war, the doctor noticed his eyes weren't as good as they should be. He was forty-three at the time, so did not mind the thought of wearing glasses. Diagnosis, however, revealed the presence of a rare disease about which little was yet known at the time.

"I talked it over with a specialist, who thought there wasn't much likelihood of its affecting the vital area of my sight, but he wasn't sure," the doctor relates. "It was a time of great testing, and caused me to prayerfully assess once again how much I needed to rely upon the Lord and not upon my own strength."

Through the intervening years, his eyesight has remained sharp, enabling the continuance of intricate surgical procedures.

But the greatest trial had yet to come, a touching of the fount of faith more demanding than any previous encounter.

One evening, as the doctor took his bath, he noticed a small patch of numbness on one toe. He did not recall having injured either of his feet in any way, and gave no particularly serious thought at the moment to the discovery, thinking the condition might clear up during the night.

"It brought an uneasiness to my mind, however," he told me, "for upon awakening the next morning, I promptly examined the toe. The numbness was still there, quite pronounced in fact, and I decided to make some tests."

Without telling his wife or any members of the staff, he slipped over to the laboratory. It was early morning, no more than a slight stir of activity about the hospital, and he slipped into the lab unnoticed. His pulse had quickened. There was a slight lack of the customary steadiness so characteristic of his hands.

For the symptoms indicated possible leprosy, a disease which usually first manifests itself in the extremities.

He did a careful diagnosis.

"My experiences as a pathologist during those years in the army had not required this type of diagnosis," he relates, "but from time to time we do have leprosy patients coming to the hospital, and I remember hearing of missionaries contracting the disease."

He checked and rechecked his findings.

Though he tried to convince himself otherwise, he was finally convinced he had con-
tracted the dread disease.

He had leprosy!

25 The doctor walked quietly through the
garden.

Morning lifted slowly out of the horizon. In
the great pipal tree, the kastura bird whistled
its final notes until another day would dawn.
A farmer's wife drove her gaunt herd of cattle
along the canal that fringed the outer edge of
the garden. In the distance, a farmer, possibly
the woman's husband, called loudly and angrily to his indolent sons, urging them to the
fields. A cool breeze, remnant from the night,
blew down from the mountains.

This is the day that the Lord hath made!

On other mornings, the doctor often quoted
this statement of praise as he walked in the
garden.

Not this morning.

The roots of his faith reached deep, wanting
to acknowledge God's purposes. A throbbing
sense of renewed intimacy with Providence
permeated his being. But the dull hurt of
anguish had turned him completely from
his customary morning optimism, his sprightly step.

Leprosy.

Please, God!

No!

The hush of night yet lay upon the courtyard, as he stepped into the hospital grounds.
A low din of voices came from the patient's
quarters, where mothers sat baking chapatis.

From Edenbagh village a half mile away came a rooster's awakening crow, a mongrel dog's plaintive reply.

A bullock cart drew up to the main gate, and the driver, seeing the doctor, vaulted out and came running.

"*Mera chhoto larka bahut bimar hai!*" the man whined, telling of the illness of his son.

By the impulse of never purposely affronting a patient, the doctor paused momentarily.

"*Nurse se ap ko bharti honi paregi pahle.*"

"*Wuh bahut hi bimar hai, Daktar Sahib.*"

The man would not be put off. The doctor must at least feel the boy's pulse. He motioned to the cart, from which the mother came, carrying the son. It was a marvel she could do it, for the lad was half as big as she, and the doctor forgot his own personal concerns in that quickly passing moment.

He felt the child's forehead, placed his fingers momentarily on the child's wrist, and then instructed the parents where to go for admittance. They walked away, pleased, chattering to each other, sure that all would be well with their son.

The doctor moved quickly now through a brief open space which separated the entrance to the main theatre and the female ward, so he could slip unnoticed into the laboratory.

"Good morning, Dr. Lehmann." The greeting was from one of the male nurses, who had been on duty during the night.

"Good morning, David."

"Is there anything I can do to help you?"

"No, thank you."

He hesitated a moment, until the male nurse had gone on in the continuation of duty, and then entered the laboratory.

He took a book from a nearby shelf, Professor Living's *Elephantrasis Graecorum or True Leprosy*, an old volume. He glanced a few moments through its pages. He selected another book, a syllabus on dermatology.

He had diagnosed numerous cases of leprosy over the years, and well knew that the disease usually manifests itself in one of three forms: nodular, smooth, or anesthetic mixed. In the first case, dark red or coppery patches form about the face, on the backs of the hands and feet, and on the body, disappearing and returning as the skin thickens, first pink and then brown.

The smooth spot on the doctor's toe fit the second description, less severe and more chronic than nodular leprosy, characterized by diminished sensitivity over affected areas of skin. In advanced stages, persons thus afflicted may suffer severe burns or cuts when the sense of touch becomes so impaired the sufferer is not aware he has come into contact with a dangerous object.

Once again, the doctor rechecked his own personal findings, hoping for some chink in his diagnosis.

There was none.

The diagnosis held firm.

Leprosy!

He slipped out of the laboratory and made his way across the back of the hospital toward the house. A number of ambulatory patients stirred about now, and several of them came to report new aches and pains suffered during the night. The doctor gave each a word of encouragement, did quick pulse checks, then hurried briskly on his way.

Once beyond the hospital compound, he

broke pace again, following the walk toward the chapel.

The children were awake, and from the veranda came their happy chatter. Inside the house, Monica was already engaged in her first responsibilities. It had been good to be with his family. Seperation during the war years had many times brought the cutting ache of loneliness to his heart.

But never in all his life had he felt such loneliness as came over him now.

He must submerge in silence the diagnosis he had made. He needed time to think, to weigh all the complex factors, to chart a plan of action.

He did not enter the chapel, but walked instead to the gate overlooking the small burial grounds, holding in rest the bodies of several Indian Christians. His eyes searched out one headstone, the English woman who, during a visit with her son at Herbertpur, had slipped away to join her husband in the Savior's presence.

A strong man, on whose shoulders rested the responsibility of one of India's great hospitals, whose mind and heart bore the widely encompassing vision of the India dream, this man needed his mother.

He looked back toward the house.

Times innumerable, Monica had brought the touch of strength he needed to face the complexities of their mission. Theirs was a marriage based on sharing. But how could he bring himself to impose upon her the shock she would so deeply feel, before it became no longer possible to shield her from it?

No, this was a road he must walk alone.

Alone?

Even as the thought crossed his mind, he felt the thrust of shame.

All things work together for good to them that love God . . . I will never leave thee nor forsake thee . . . Trust in the Lord with all thine heart and lean not onto thine own understanding.

"Dear Lord," he whispered, "there is so much I have to learn of what it means to trust Thee. Teach me, Lord, whatever the price may be."

Peace came to his heart, though the weight remained, and he understood. He would walk through a long and lonely valley, but the Shepherd would lead the way.

The Lord is my shepherd.

What a blessed thought!

He made his way back to the house, and the children on the veranda, catching sight of him, came running and laughing, each wanting to be swept up into his arms.

Dare he touch them?

Oh God, he breathed heavenward, *do what you must to better fit me for your service, but spare the children!*

Entering the house, he called out, "Monica!" He was pleased to hear the customary pleasantness in his voice.

"On the back veranda, Geoffrey."

He went to her.

"My, you were up early," she said, not looking away from the sheaf of correspondence she was answering.

"I didn't sleep too well," he said.

She looked up.

"Are you ill?"

"I feel fine, but I've had a number of things on my mind."

"You oughtn't to let anything spoil your sleep," she scolded. She was never abrasive when she expressed opposition or reprimand, her prime concern being always for his best and the good of the work.

He walked to the open side of the veranda. It was fully screened, looking out onto the garden, and he and Monica spent many pleasant moments in relaxation here.

"Is there anything I can do to help?" she asked.

He didn't reply.

She continued writing, pausing after a few moments to say, "There is a very touching letter here from a dear man who was converted at the hospital. He was that man one of our workers found out in the jungle, living with scarcely anything to eat. Shall I read it to you?"

The doctor turned. "Yes, please," he said.

"His handwriting is quite poor, so it is a bit difficult to make out. He had had very little schooling as I remember, but it's beautiful, the way his thoughts are expressed here. He says, 'My constant prayer is that He may please guide us to glorify His name on this earth, as His name is glorified in heaven. When we talk, let us talk of Him. When we listen, let us listen to Him. When we act, let us act for Him. Let us die for Him.' Isn't that remarkable?"

The doctor made no comment, for God was using the letter to minister deeply to his heart. Suppose there had never been a Herbertpur Mission Hospital? Suppose he had remained in England, to forge a fortune in steel? Had not God, in His sovereignty, brought them to India so that this man's doxology might come forth from a jungle of sin and despair?

Dare he question, so much as for a moment or in the face of any circumstance, but what this same God watched over him now?

"You are very quiet," his wife said.

"Just thinking."

"About the letter?"

"Yes."

"It's very beautiful. What a blessing to know the Lord touches hearts like that through our ministry."

The doctor walked to a wicker chair near his wife, and sat down.

"When we go shopping in Dehra Dun tomorrow, let's be sure to see the travel agent. We must not let ourselves become so busy this summer we don't take time to slip home for a short furlough."

"I've just written a letter to Prilla and Peta," Mrs. Lehmann said. "It's so lonely for them at school. I'll add a note telling them of our plans."

So, a move at a time, the doctor carefully plotted his course.

Word was spread among the patients that the doctor would be gone for several weeks during the hot season, and as the time for departure drew near, the daily stream of patients grew to the point where it was almost impossible to see all of them. But it was good. He needed a maelstrom of activity to insulate his mind from thoughts of himself.

Not that he ignored his physical problem. He kept careful watch of his condition. The spot on his toe remained anesthetized, but it remained the same, and no other manifestations of the disease appeared.

The control and cure of leprosy had advanced even beyond the blessed discovery of chaulmoogra oil, and medication in the earliest stages might quickly restore him to full health. He debated initiating the treatment himself, but the trip back to England would make possible consultation with an old friend, a leprologist, recognized throughout the world for his research skill, and so long as he detected no spread of the disease, it seemed best to wait.

The deepest hurt came when he thought of being separated from his family.

It is one of the darkest vales a missionary walks, separation from his children. There was no provision whatever for the Lehmann children to receive their education at Herbertpur, once they became ten years of age, and so they were sent to England. At such times it becomes necessary for harvest-land parents to convince their children that they, too, are missionaries.

Too often the Lehmanns had seen missionary children growing apart from the faith of their parents, since separation so often fosters spiritual rebellion. It was to be their joy through the years to again and again thank God for children who, through years of loneliness, kept respect for their parents and found for themselves an enduring faith.

Yet, for all a man may love his children, the greatest price is separation from his wife. This, as the doctor well knew, would be the case if he were committed to a leprosarium.

Since childhood, he had loved islands, and he thought how odd that he might be spending a portion of his life on one, thus alienated from the world.

But, whatever, he grew strong in the confidence that God had a reason for every event in his life, and he prayed for the strength and the courage to face this crisis, whatever the outcome might be.

The trip back to England was a thrilling time, being united with Priscilla and Peta, the fellowship of Christian friends. But the doctor had one foremost objective. This he dispatched, secretly, at the earliest opportunity.

"Only this one spot?" the leprologist asked, examining the toe.

"That's all," the doctor told him. "I've been quite encouraged in that respect."

The leprologist continued his examination, quietly for a moment. Then he said, "You have reason to be much more encouraged."

"Why is that?"

"My diagnosis is that this is only a skin lesion."

"Not leprosy?"

"Not leprosy."

Subsequent tests confirmed the initial report. The doctor, invariably inerrant in the diagnosis of patients at Herbertpur, had been wrong in the calculation of his own personal condition.

Thank God!

26 My first visit to Herbertpur, in the autumn of 1964, was meaningful to me in a number of ways.

Off and on during the previous two or three years, my wife and I had made plans for our twenty-fifth wedding anniversary, which fell on the sixteenth of November. When the call of duty led me back to the Orient, though I had been there on a similar assignment earlier that year, my wife was in full and enthusiastic agreement. She would remain at home, keeping watch over the business.

So we celebrated our twenty-fifth anniversary under unusual circumstances.

She was with her mother in Nebraska, not realizing we would also be seperated the following year as, on our anniversary date, the last page was turned in the volume of her mother's life.

While my wife was feted to a special dinner in America, the Lehmanns planned an Indian feast for me, removing table and chairs and silverware from the dining room, so we could sit on the floor and partake with our bare hands.

But I was not alone.

Our son, Lane, had joined me at Herbertpur, together with Dan Dunkelberger, production manager for our organization. The three of us had been together in Hong Kong working on our film, *Inhale the Incense*, and I had gone on ahead to India while they looked after a number of shooting assignments for several documentary films we were making along the way.

The night before Dan and Lane arrived, a young man was brought down out of the hills. He was eighteen years of age, the same as our son, and had been carried for thirty hours by an uncle and a brother and two neighbors.

I was not aware of his coming, however, until after Dr. Lehmann and I drove back from Dehra Dun, having met the newcomers at the train.

Shortly after our arrival, Dan, Lane and I slipped over to the hospital. Dr. Warlow, at work in surgery, sent word for us to put on sterile clothes and come in.

"I've got something here you'll find very interesting," he said.

The young man brought down from the hills during the night, lay on the operating table.

"Frankly," Dr. Warlow said, "I could use a little help, and it might be good to have some photos, if you would care to do so."

He motioned for us to come closer, and we first saw an enormous flesh wound in the boy's thigh.

"What happened?" one of us asked.

"He was attacked by one of those treacherous Himalayan bears," the doctor told us. "His most serious injury is his face."

We looked.

And for a moment looked away!

It was not a face. It was a skull breathing. Nose and upper lip completely torn away. The top scalp laid fully open.

The doctor told us what he knew of the mishap.

The young man had been out herding his goats, when a full-sized Himalayan bear, conceded by zoologists to be the most treacherous and ferocious of all species, lunged out of the brush. In a matter of seconds, he struck down the boy, rolled him in the dirt, clawed at him without mercy. Then, impulsively, he turned and snatched one of the goats, killing it in an instant, and disappeared.

"It's incredible, the stamina of this chap," the doctor told us. My son and I held his mangled leg, as the doctor's hand all but disappeared, reaching in to clean debris out of the immense wound. "He's in a state of considerable shock, and he has lost blood terribly, but his pulse is quite good."

I watched my son, the deep sense of identification that came to his face, and prayed he might not only be moved by the physical side of missions, but also sense the far deeper implications.

"This kid might never have heard the Gospel except for this experience, Lane," I whispered.

"Yeah, Dad," he mumbled, "How about that?"

The three of us remained at Herbertpur for two more days, and kept close watch on the progress of the lad from the hills.

One evening, as we talked about the obvious need for plastic surgery, Dr. Warlow said, "We can't handle it here. What I would like to do is send him to a hospital where they do a good deal of this type of thing. It won't be easy."

"Too expensive?" I asked.

"For these people it would be quite expensive," he said, "but that's not the only problem. The hill folk are so reluctant to venture away from the hills."

"What's the most it might cost?" I asked.

"Fifteen thousand rupees, perhaps twenty thousand at the most."

Later that evening, alone in our room, Lane said, "Twenty thousand rupees is less than five thousand bucks, Dad. Maybe our family could take this up as a project. I'd be willing to pay up to half of it myself."

Dr. Warlow liked the idea, and the three of us went to the hospital to talk with the young lad's relatives. The doctor explained what would need to be done, and soon the men were chattering among themselves.

After listening a moment, Dr. Warlow turned to us and said, "The usual thing is happening here. What they are saying is that this is their hospital and I am their doctor and no one anyplace else could do any more for the boy than we can do. It is so hard to get these people to see that there are some things we really shouldn't attempt here at Herbertpur."

He talked with the men for another moment. Then he turned to us and said, "They can't seem to understand how a face, once completely gone, could ever come back again. They are fatalists, these people, and they feel that if this is what the gods have permitted, then there is nothing they can do about it."

A thought came to my mind. Dan, our production manager, had nearly lost a finger some years before he came to work with us, and the doctors temporarily fastened the injured digit to his abdomen, using the flesh from his body to build a new finger. I asked Lane to fetch Dan, so we could give these men a tangible illustration of what the doctor was talking about.

It is a scene we will always remember, the wonderment of these men as the doctor showed them the large scar on Dan's abdomen and then, explaining what had happened, let them carefully examine the restored finger.

"Their attitude has changed considerably now," Dr. Warlow said. "Let's invite them over to the house. I have a book on plastic surgery which may convince them further."

At the house, the men sat characteristically on the floor, as the doctor brought out the volume he had mentioned, and showed them before and after photographs of lip and nasal restorations.

If the dawn of knowledge upon the human mind is a dramatic event, and it surely is, then it was an awesome moment as we watched these humble hill men peer beyond the precipice of their little world. The doctor, in whom they placed implicit trust, had opened the cover of a book. They looked at that book in transfixed wonder. It was like opening the door into the world of newspapers and radio and television and all the kindred wonders of which these men had spoken as the ancients once spoke of the stars.

They talked loudly among themselves for several moments, pointing to the pictures in the book but seemingly oblivious of us.

"What are they saying?" I asked.

"It's quite interesting, really," the doctor replied. "One of them just said it can't be possible to give a man back his face, and the other said, 'You saw it in the doctor's book, didn't you?' And so they're all pretty much convinced it could happen."

In a bit, the men looked up. How much would be the cost of so wondrous a thing?

The doctor told them, and their faces clouded with dismay. Quickly, the doctor asked how much they might be able to contribute themselves, and once again they huddled in conference.

Their answer, amazing to all of us, was five hundred rupees!

"That is a tremendous amount of money to these people," Dr. Warlow said, "but what they would do is pool their resources. These people live somewhat as clans, you know, and they stand together in times like this."

Five hundred rupees! One could not think of it simply as a hundred dollars. What did it really compare to in contrast to Western affluence? Ten thousand dollars? Twenty-five? Perhaps fifty thousand?

"Shouldn't you tell them, Dad?" Lane whispered.

Dr. Warlow heard him and said, "That's what I'm about to do. I want to be sure I frame my words properly. It's terribly hard sometimes to get these hill people to understand us."

The doctor now turned to the hill men, speaking to them in deliberate phrases, repeating frequently in response to their questions. Slowly, it came to them that we were friends, that we wanted to help them. If they would send this boy to a government hospital, we would furnish as much money as might be needed above the five hundred rupees they could supply.

Impulsively, the boy's older brother, a man I judged to be in his late twenties, moved over to my chair and prostrated himself on the floor as though in worship.

"You are our *Bhagwan!*" he exclaimed in the language of the hills.

"It is a common thing," Dr. Warlow said, "for hill people to ascribe deity to someone who has greatly befriended them."

In a foolish moment, some men might have revelled in it, the thought of being called "God" by another human being. But I remembered the tetanus patient. I thought of the many groping minds for whom *Bhagwan* was anything from a monstrous, nefarious creature belching fire from his nostrils to a nymph-like presence capable of bestowing great good, if only mortals could spell out the proper incantation whereby to summon his attention.

With Dr. Warlow interpreting, we gave our witness. We told these men of our own spiritual unworthiness apart from the mercy of God. And I felt again that sense of meaning which must come to every missionary as he brings Light to those who have known only darkness.

As a result of the evening's conversation, our "bear boy," as we have come to call him, went to a government hospital some five hundred miles distant. During the interim, when I returned the following March to join Heinz Fussle in the filming of *Tashi from Tibet*, Dr. Warlow made repeated efforts to obtain information relative to the lad's condition. But like all hospitals in India, the government hospital is overworked and understaffed and officials, not realizing the depth of our emotional involvement in the case, did not take the time to reply.

But the "bear boy" will one day return to Herbertpur and so the chapter is not closed. For God is at work among the hill people, the people of the Jaunsar, and our "bear boy" must surely be another channel the doctors and the staff will utilize to bring the message of hope and redemption to these intriguing, colorful people.

In our hearts there is a frequent prayer that, one day in the sunless brilliance of the Redeemer's throne, we shall see the "bear boy" with a restored countenance and a soul set free.

Oh God, may it be so!

27 Two days after the "bear boy" experience, the three of us said good-bye to Herbertpur. We had a filmstrip assignment to complete in Pakistan, after which Dan Dunkelberger returned to India for final photography on a missionary documentary.

But in the spring of 1964, Heinz Fussle returned to India to set up production of the dramatic film *Tashi from Tibet,* sponsored by Dr. Lehmann. I joined him in March, and we pursued the project until May. Though much of the work was done up in the mountains, against the backdrop ot the Tibetan border, we made our base at the hospital, and spent many memorable days with the Lehmanns and the Warlows and the others at the hospital whose friendship we had come to so deeply cherish.

The very nature of the project put us into close proximity with several hundred Tibetans, a story all its own. Through the years, Tibetans have come to the hospital. In no large number, by virtue of the fact that few Tibetans ever ventured beyond the snows prior to the Chinese invasion, but in ample numbers to keep these clever, majestic people high on the list of items for prayer.

The people of Tibet were people of the hills, thus part of the India dream. As chairman of the board of governors at Wynberg-Allen schools, the doctor had worked closely with missionaries of the Evangelical Alliance Mission, the organization that pioneered ministry along Tibet's frontier. Also, the Lehmanns shared close friendship with Rev. and Mrs. E. T. Phunthsog, two of the world's most outstanding Tibetans.

The previous autumn, the doctor had taken

me to the Phunthsog's home, a pleasant cottage on a scenic ravine winding down from the Himalayas, and I had barely stepped inside the door when I recognized a photograph of Yoseb Gergan. Gergan's father, private secretary to the Panchen Lama, had fled for his life from Lhasa, accused of plotting the death of the Dalai Lama.

Sonam Gergan, though an avowed Buddhist, assisted two Moravian missionaries in the translation of the Tibetan Bible, a task he never lived to complete. As a mere boy, his son Yoseb secretly read the manuscript for the Gospel of John and, as a result, became a believer.

It was Yoseb Gergan who devoted his entire life to the completion of the Tibetan Bible.

Mrs. E. T. Phunthsog is the daughter of Yoseb Gergan. Her husband, a prominent man among Tibetans, contemplated becoming a lama, heard the Gospel and believed. Without his excellent rapport with the Dalai Lama and the exiled Tibetan Government, we could never have produced our film.

The outflow of love members of the hospital staff expressed to Champa, the young Tibetan chosen to portray Tashi, vividly demonstrated the feelings of these people toward the spiritual needs of all who live in the high country. Champa became like a member of the Lehmanns' family, like a son and a brother to those of us who worked with him.

Increasingly now, Tibetans come to Herbertpur. Tashi's eye surgery is, in fact, based on the actual experience of a Tibetan brought to Herbertpur, his eyes blinded by an explosion.

But, except for refugees, the people of Tibet

continue to live far removed from the hospital, imprisoned now within the wall of iron forged by the Communists. So it is the Jaunsari tribes, the beloved hill people, who benefit most frequently. It is the Jaunsaris who lie so very close to the doctor's heart.

And it is the Jaunsaris who yet walk in darkness, shut off by superstition and ignorance from the Gospel message.

In any missionary outreach, the great need is for liaison. Through the years, the doctor and his staff had established many-friendly contacts among the Jaunsaris, none more helpful than a captivating gentleman named Joshi, a well-educated Jaunsari Brahmin devoting his life to the betterment of the people. Joshi is a brilliant young man, a teacher. He has an open and inquiring mind. He has spent many hours talking with Dr. Lehmann about the Christian faith.

I have seen the doctor moved to the point of tears, as he told me of his appreciation and respect for Joshi, and of the desire deep in his heart that this leader of his people may one day commit his life to the Savior and become, as well he could be, an apostle to the hills.

With the clash of border incidents between Indian and Chinese troops, much of the hill area has been zoned by the military, and closed to visitors. This includes Chakrata, the idyllic hill village where the Lehmanns established the dispensary they were forced to close for shortage of personnel.

Residents of Chakrata, such as Joshi, are permitted to come freely to the lowlands. Joshi, hearing of our desire to build a sequence around some of the brightly-costumed folk dancers, offered to bring a group down to a small Jaunsari settlement just below the military line.

Early that morning, Champa, Heinz Fussle and I, with Dr. Lehmann as our driver and guide, headed out toward the hills in the hospital Land Rover to a predetermined meeting place along the road from the mountains.

Our journey took us through tiger-inhabited jungle, though it being daylight, we kept our cameras ready in vain for the possible appearance of one of the cats.

A few evenings earlier, we had gone with the Lehmanns to meet a *shikari*, as hunters are called in the area, a bed-ridden Britisher who had lived for many years in a planter's house directly alongside the sacred Jamuna.

Directly above his bed hung an enlarged photograph of a huge tiger, slain in the very area through which we traveled on our way to the Jaunsari settlement.

"Did you shoot the tiger?" I asked.

There must have been a touch of naivety in the way I spoke, for he winked slyly and said, "No, sir, I strangled him to death!"

Joshi and his colorful entourage met us at the appointed intersection, and the doctor transported us a load at a time to the base of a steep incline. Up along the hillside we would find a small cluster of Jaunsari farmers.

I had, of course, seen many of the Jaunsaris at the hospital. One evening Dr. Lehmann took us to the living quarters provided for family members of those hospitalized. One large room quartered some twenty or more Jaunsaris. At sight of their beloved doctor, they laughed and chattered in delight. He sat on the floor in their midst, clapping rhythm as they sang several of their mountain ballads. Then he patiently taught them the lyrics and melody of a Gospel hymn.

I looked forward with keen anticipation to seeing these people in their own locale.

The heat of the sun was merciless, as we carried our equipment up to the settlement from as far as the Land Rover could go, and then set up our camera and reflectors and, with the help of Joshi, told our colorful "extras" what was expected of them in the film sequence.

It was a long day, with many opportunities to talk about the people of the hills.

They live near the headwaters of the Jamuna. The sacred Ganges likewise draws its first waters from these hills, since the Jamuna is one of its tributaries. Fed by the eternal snows, cascading streams become the arteries of life for the central plains of India and Pakistan.

As these many streams flow down out of the mountains and through the lower hills, they divide the high country into hundreds of sections, each of which is inhabited by *Paharis*, or hill tribes. These people, having much in common, are never the less divided so strictly by the river boundries that they have separate names, habits, language, and costume.

"They are a lovable people," the doctor told me. "They have a simple sense of humor, rather like my own, as my children say, a prep school type of joking. In fact, my simple jokes go very well with them."

In contrast to the men of the plains, especially the Muslims who so frequently mistreat their wives, women of the hills receive preferential treatment. For one thing, there is traditionally an acute shortage of women, so that the practice of polyandry has developed.

"The men proudly introduce their wives at the hospital," Dr. Lehmann says. "I've seen a man get down on the floor to put a pair of new shoes on his wife's feet, when she has had a prolonged stay with us. I've also seen a hill man standing outside the operating theatre in tears as we took his wife to surgery."

One day an old hill man staggered into the compound carrying his wife in a large basket on his back, having traversed a distance of some thirty miles.

Marital bliss has its inclement moments, however.

Women of the hills wear pierced jewelry in their noses and in their ears. A useful habit, Jaunsari men say, because a woman who does not obey her husband can be reprimanded by giving a good pull to the ring in her nose.

The doctor learned in the earliest days of Herbertpur, however, that loud shouting between these hill people does not necessarily mean a quarrel. On the occasion of one heated argument, he suggested to a man looking on that they ought to do something to separate the two in disagreement.

"But Sahib," the man said, "they are not angry. They are discussing whether it will rain today."

Early habitants of the hills seem to have come as Aryan migrants from the west, giving the Jaunsaris a higher proportion of Aryan blood than any other caste or tribe in India.

As a nation, India is making a heroic effort to stamp out the caste system. But the people of the hills live far removed from the touch of social reformers.

Dr. Lehmann tells of an occasion when he came into one of the wards and saw a hill woman cooking food beside one of the beds.

"I'm sorry," he said to her, "but we cannot allow cooking in the ward. You must do your cooking outside."

The next morning, he found her once again at her little stove and, lest she had misunderstood him before, took considerable pains to make sure she now knew what he meant.

On the third morning, however, she was still there. Irritated, he scooped up the kettle and small charcoal stove and carried them some distance away in the courtyard.

"A near crisis erupted," he recalls. "This woman was of a high caste and I polluted her kettle by touching it, making it necessary for her to go without food for quite some time. I was, of course, very sorry."

On another occasion up in the hills, the doctor and his wife had been trekking from village to village with some national co-workers on an evangelistic effort.

"I walk more quickly than most," the doctor says, "and so I arrived in the village ahead of the others. A couple of people sat talking near the center of the village, so I joined them. They invited me to sit down, and then one man pointed toward a stone, and I supposed he meant for me to sit on it. This I did."

What the man had actually done, however, was to invite the doctor to sit but, by all means, not to sit on the stone, since it was the habitation of their most prominent god.

"Though they were quite disturbed," the doctor says, "they were much too polite to ask me to get off the stone. Instead, the head man sent one of the boys to his house for a chair, and I didn't quite understand the reason until our co-workers arrived."

The hill people love their hospital and the people who look after them. They are so eager to please that diagnosis is sometimes hindered by the patient's desire to reply in the manner he thinks most pleasing to the doctor.

One man, asked to provide a specimen, could not at the moment do so. Lest he disappoint the doctor, he brought in a mixture of water and cow dung.

They love the *melas,* which occur frequently during the winter months, and congregate in great numbers to sing and dance and consume huge quantities of mutton and home-made liquor, the latter being perhaps their greatest failing.

"Literacy among women is almost unknown," the doctor says, "and very low among men. The government is making a determined effort to correct this. Sometime ago, before military action closed the hills to us, we were asked to take part in a village *mela.* At the end of a short talk, I offered Gospel portions for sale. We were literally mobbed for these, selling fifty in a few minutes and having visitors all that evening asking for more."

A number of young people, such as Joshi, have gone out of the hills to study. At least one girl has promised to bring medicine back to her people.

Jaunsari women dress beautifully. Their costume consists of a voluminous skirt made from some six yards of material hanging to the ankles, colorfully bordered. Their skirts sway gracefully as the women walk. A close-fitting coat, with colored edging, is worn

231

in winter. Nose rings are worn by even the most poor among the women, and sometimes as many as ten rings are attached to the ears.

The poorer people make their rings of silver, but the more wealthy wear gold rings, in some cases worth thousands of rupees. These are the hill man's bank account, drawn upon only in an emergency.

While quite young, Jaunsari bodies are delicately tatooed with flowers, gods and formal designs.

Men wear a simple loin cloth, a shirt, and on their heads a tight-fitting beret with a rolled edge. They present an appearance far less colorful than do the women.

During that day of filming, I was especially struck by the design of the houses. Built up on rocky ledges, usually made of stone, their sloping roofs constructed of large stone slabs. The houses vary in design from simple one-roomed dwellings of the low classes to the elaborate stone and wood domiciles of wealthy land owners. These latter structures have graceful wooden pillars, with Gothic-type arches. The woodwork is painted in bright colors.

Livestock, mostly cattle, occupy the ground floor. Being strict Hindus, Jaunsaris do not eat beef. The cattle provide milk and, in the absence of oxen, sometimes serve as dray animals.

We were led up a narrow stone staircase to the interior of one house. It had such a low ceiling, we could not stand erect. There was no furniture. Jaunsaris eat and sit and sleep on the floor. An open cooking hearth, surrounded by what seemed to be a high mud base, dominated the center of the main room.

232

I marveled that such procedure would not cause numerous house burnings.

In cases of the practice of polyandry, children call each of the brother husbands *baba*, since there is obviously an uncle relationship. Each brother, except the eldest, has a prefix to the name *baba*, relating his occupational position in the family. *Bakra Baba*, for example, denotes the father who looks after the goats.

The wife cannot be selected from the same village or *Khut*, as adjacent villages are called. She is generally married at the age of seven or eight, and betrothed even younger. The *Jaldha*, which is the betrothal fee, ranges from one to five rupees. The bridal price, however, is likely to be much higher.

Often one sees a rather pathetic little figure, dressed in all her finery, with her small bridal party of perhaps three or four, wending their way across the hills to the bridegroom's house.

Sometimes, in the case of rich landowners or *Sayanas*, village men who hold semi-judiciary powers, the *barat* as the bridal party is called, may consist of as many as five hundred people. In such instances, fifty goats may be killed to provide food at the feast.

Only half of the bridal price is paid at the time of the marriage. If the wife is childless, her parents will be required to return the amount. When the first child is born, however, the full price is paid.

Divorce frequently occurs, at which time the parents, or the new husband or husbands, pay back the original bride price. If the wife has borne several children, the amount may be greatly increased.

"The wife has the privilege during festivals of returning to her own village," Dr. Lehmann told us. "Here she is known as *Dhanti*, and is allowed great freedom, even license. If, as sometimes happens, the man on whom she has chosen to bestow her favors is more pleasing to her than her husband, she has the right to stay with him if he is willing to pay the divorce fees. While I certainly do not approve of such customs, it is easy to see that a husband, who wishes to retain his wife, must learn to please her, at least for some months before the next festival."

The Jaunsaris are avowed animists. They attribute supernatural powers to many trees and rocks and other forms of nature. Magic, too, wields a strong influence over their lives. They believe in witches and the power of the evil eye. The *mela*, with all its singing and dancing, drinking and gaiety, into which they so wholeheartedly throw themselves, is a time when they believe the gods permit them to escape from the fear and hardship surrounding their lives.

"At Chakrata, where we established a dispensary," the doctor told me, "the government built a small hospital. It was not very popular. When I visited it some years ago, there were no inpatients, and very few operations performed. We ran our dispensary five months during the summer, being careful not to promote our work in any way. Even so, the numbers rose so rapidly we were soon seeing more than a hundred a day. One day we actually saw over two hundred and fifty patients. We attributed this very clearly as the blessing of God upon our efforts."

"It's tragic you had to close the dispensary

at Chakrata," I said. "Wasn't it an ideal center for evangelism?"

"It certainly was," the doctor replied soberly. "Our problem, as I've said before, was we simply did not have sufficient personnel to maintain both the hospital at Herbertpur and the dispensary in the hills."

"You have said hill people not only listen intently to the Gospel, but are also deeply touched by it."

"This is true."

"Then if you had been able to maintain the dispensary at Chakrata, is it not possible your spiritual ministry might be far more fruitful? Isn't it a disadvantage only being able to contact them when they come down to the hospital?"

"Without a doubt," the doctor replied, a quiet sadness on his face. "If somehow we could maintain a continuous ministry among these people, we would see more definite results. As you know, they often come down to the hospital as outpatients. But they only remain for a few days. They hear the Gospel. If they are literate, they may take back something to read. But it is very difficult to lead a man out of spiritual darkness, unless you can spend time with him."

I asked, "Doesn't a situation like this add up to an indictment of the Christian Church?"

"I'm afraid so, Ken," the doctor said. "A virile church should produce enough missionaries just as a strong nation fields sufficient soldiers. The Jaunsaris are only one group needing to be reached. There are thousands more. But the Church simply isn't supplying harvesters. I wonder sometimes if it's our fault as missionaries."

"Your fault?"

"Perhaps missionaries do not adequately convey to the Church at home the magnitude of opportunity."

"I think it may be true that, in some respects, missionaries fail to express the enthusiasm they feel inside. By and large, though, the fault lies with Christians themselves, putting material interests above spiritual interests. They numb their minds so they cannot perceive spiritual opportunity. The Bible says *beware of covetousness, which is idolatry,* and what does a man covet more than material comfort? Which means, when you come right down to it, some people are just as idolatrous as these Jaunsaris. Education and exposure to Christianity have removed supersitition, but it's idolatry just the same."

It was a great day spent among the Jaunsaris. Getting to know Joshi better, visiting one of the colorful homes, filming a bit of the gaiety of the hills. But as we made our way back to the Land Rover and then along the snaking jungle trail to the main Chakrata highway, confusing and tormenting thoughts beset my heart and mind. Had we not done more than photography this sweltering day? Was not the paper dryness of my tongue more than a physical thirst?

I thought of the "bear boy" episode of the previous autumn, of the wonder in the eyes of those Jaunsari men when Dr. Warlow opened the medical book and gave them a glimpse of a world unknown. This day I had looked intimately into the world of the Jaunsar.

Even as young Jaunsaris, led by such fine champions for the better life as Joshi, yearned to know more of my world, why could it not be possible to somehow stir indolent hearts within the Church to hunger for a knowledge of the world of the Jaunsar? A hunger to help, to bring the Light of Christ, to discover the rewarding joys of dedication and stewardship as the doctor and his staff had done.

What could I do — it was a flaming cry within my heart — to help awaken the Church to its sublime opportunities?

28 Dr. Lehmann has an aversion to small talk. He is likely to excuse himself from visitors whose conversation seldom ventures beyond the weather and life's mundane moments. But asked a lead question on such topics as theology or philosophy, and the doctor sparkles with interest and conversation.

Nothing, however, draws him out more quickly than the subject of missionary medicine as a tool for evangelism.

"I simply cannot understand the thinking of medical missionaries who content themselves with ministering only to the physical needs," he told me. "It is true Christ commissioned us to *heal the sick*, but He also said *preach the Gospel*. This was no afterthought. By ministering to a man's body, we prepare the way for touching his deeper spiritual need."

I never heard him speak in outright judgment of doctors and nurses who come to the mission field, and devote their full time to medicine. Some lack the innate capacity for good communication. The doctor knows this. Yet the tenacity of his convictions strongly indicates impatience with those who, for whatever reason, fail to see medicine's ideal role as a harvest implement.

"We give all diligence to make sure our equipment and techniques meet the highest possible specifications," he says. "It is a thrilling thing to see health restored. But, at best, a man's physical body is temporal. His eternal soul must be our first concern. We must help these people to see themselves not just as so many human beings but as a part of God's eternal plan."

From their earliest days in India, the doctor and his wife envisioned medical missions as a four-pronged aid to evangelism.

First, medicine brings people to a central place, where they can effectively hear the Gospel. In the past, a white man could go anywhere and gather a crowd of listeners. Today, rampant nationalism has changed this.

"As I have told you," the doctor said, "we have a hundred villages within a five mile radius of our hospital. Small though this area is, it would take us months to visit these villages. Yet in one morning, on almost any given day, medicine gives us the opportunity to communicate our faith to multitudes of people who come to our hospital from these villages, as well, of course, as places much farther away, including closed areas, such as Tibet, where we could never enter.

"I remember one very sick man who came to the hospital. He had been spending the last years of his life in contemplation, living in an inaccessible cave in the hills on the other side of the Jamuna River. We diagnosed his case as incurable, and kept him at the hospital for the last few weeks of his life, so we might make him more comfortable.

"This unknown man became the center of our attention. We did everything we could to ease his suffering. But, as you well know, our even greater concern was to help him see what Christ had done for him. Before he died, he confessed before the other patients that he was trusting in the Lord Jesus for salvation. How unlikely it was that anyone would ever have brought the Gospel to his cave."

The second point in the doctor's thesis is that medicine not only brings large numbers of people to a central point, where they can be evangelized, but the use of medicine itself prepares the heart. Herbertpur case files contain numerous examples of patients who have come to the hospital suspicious, caustic, demanding, and have left in gentleness, their hearts having been deeply touched by the competence and the love of the medical staff.

In village evangelism, the missionary may have attention one moment, only to lose it in the next. At Herbertpur, *the Jesus Hospital,* patients and visitors expect to hear the Gospel. If for no other reason, they listen out of appreciation.

The doctor's fourth argument for medical missions is that it opens closed doors and establishes rapport in the most difficult villages.

"Those of us who have done village evangelism know what it is like to be driven out of a community," he told me. "Opposition can become quite violent. One day we began a Gospel service in a village some thirty miles from Herbertpur. The head man came to us and angrily commanded us to leave. He was quite adamant, until one of the villagers came and whispered, 'It is Doctor Sahib from the hospital.' Instantly, the head man's attitude changed. He not only welcomed us, but treated us as special guests.

"On many occasions, as we go into a village, former patients join the crowd of listeners, and openly speak up to support our witness. Some of them are so enthusiastic, we cannot but feel that, in spite of the little they know about the Gospel, they have come to a personal knowledge of our Savior."

The more we talked, the more I realized how encompassing stewardship had become to the doctor's total view of his life. He was in every sense of the word God's businessman, determined to make the investment of everything he had produce spiritual fruit in the hearts of his Herbertpur people. I thought of the image so many Americans have of one who witnesses. To them, a witness is some kind of starry-eyed, trauma-inflicted individual who escapes from the realities of this world by incessantly talking about the golden boulevards of the world to come. Here was a man of this earth who saw his witness as his greatest possession.

It was most invigorating.

"What is the basic philosophy of your witness here?" I asked.

"Simplicity," the doctor replied. "We try to help a man understand five things. Who is Jesus Christ? He is the Son of God. What did He do? He left his home in heaven and came down to earth. Why did He do this? To save us from our sins. How? By giving His life for us on the cross of Calvary, and coming forth victorious from the grave as eternal evidence of God's power and love. What must we do? Come to our senses, realize the awfulness of sin, repent and trust in His finished work on the cross for our salvation."

"The hospital reaches more than the poor and the illiterate, doesn't it?"

"Very definitely. We have quite a number of what one might call upper-class patients, including Maharajas and Maharanis, and we have had wonderful opportunities of telling them about Christ. My wife is particularly good at chatting with these people."

"Isn't the multiplicity of languages quite a problem?"

"It is one of our greatest problems. Most of the patients who come to the hospital understand enough Hindi or Urdu so we can get by, but when we want to present effective Christian witness, we must use the language with which the patient is most familiar."

"How about the tape recordings you play over the hospital speaker system?"

"They are indispensable. I'm always thrilled whenever I see a patient's face light up, as he hears his own familiar tongue on one of the loudspeakers."

"Like the Tibetan man brought into the hospital this morning?"

The doctor nodded. "We have several excellent tapes in Tibetan. But, of course, nothing takes the place of being able to sit quietly by a patient's bed, and either read to him from the Bible or from some Christian literature, and chat with him about his spiritual needs. Fortunately, among those on the staff, we have a number who can converse effectively in several languages.

"For those who can read, literature provides a very effective witness. From the very beginning of our ministry, we have emphasized literature. In recent years we have grown especially concerned about the fact that Communists are sending tons of literature into the country. Because of this, because of our concern to do something to effectively meet this challenge, we began the publication of our new cartoon pamphlets which you have seen."

"I am very much impressed with them," I said. "I wish I could read them."

"We keep them very simple, telling as much of the story by pictures as we possibly can."

"What kind of response do you see to literature distribution?"

"Never as much as we would like, of course. We have no way of knowing what happens in the hearts of patients who go back to their villages. We do know that, with so little reading material, they treasure even the smallest pamphlet. I recall one man who came to the hospital with a book he had purchased fifteen years before. I asked if he understood the message of the book. His eyes brightened as he told me he not only understood, but had personally trusted Christ."

"Are the *Arya Samajists* your worst obstacles to evangelism?"

"They are certainly formidable," the doctor said. "Opposition of this type frequently backfires, however, implementing rather than impeding the work of the missionary."

One morning, as the doctor walked from his house to the hospital, he heard a loud clamor coming from the worker's quarters. Quickly changing his course, he came upon a small mob shouting and waving sticks.

When the doctor at last quieted them, he

found they weren't angry because one of the men, even though he was a Brahmin, had been baptised. They objected because his wife had been brought in and, according to their accusation, was being forced into becoming a Christian.

"I explained to them that we don't force Christianity on anyone, that this had to be the work of the Holy Spirit. Surely it was right for a man's wife to hear the same things that had come to be so meaningful to her husband. Then, to help them make sure she was not being forced into anything against her wishes, I suggested they leave observers at the compound to check up on us. As a result, the leader of the opposition himself remained and, hearing the Gospel taught to the new convert's wife, also became a believer.

"I think what discourages us more than any outward opposition we face is the lack of conviction of sin among the people."

"Why is this?" I asked.

"They lack discipline. It is shocking to see the way children are allowed to have their own way, especially boys. Young boys are practically never punished. They grow up without any real concept of what it means to face the penalty for doing wrong. They simply don't think of themselves as sinners."

"I suppose even their vocabulary is a problem, isn't it?" I asked.

"Well, they certainly don't have a vocabulary orientated toward Christianity, as is the case in the West." He thought a moment. "We say a good deal, don't we, when we speak of the King's English?

"But it's more than this. Christian influence is a cumulative thing. It goes on from generation to generation. How does one speak of God's love, God's holiness, mercy and forgiveness to a man who has absolutely no concept of God at all? We don't just suddenly illuminate his mind to these staggering concepts."

"You open a subject which has been on my mind of late," I said. "The Holy Spirit works within a frame of reference. Don't you agree?"

"I surely do! And that's the whole point of our work here at the hospital. God helping us, we must demonstrate living Christianity, so these dear, blinded people can see faith in action. Little by little, they begin to understand. But it's a painfully slow process."

"It's a bit aside from the subject," I said, "but as I've watched the crowds in the hospital courtyard, there have been occasional instances of lost tempers. In my country, a lost temper usually leads to blasphemous invectives. But you know, Dr. Lehmann, these people here, who don't even know God, will never be held guilty of taking His name in vain."

"That's an interesting thought. We have examples where our patients actually belittle the Lord. Completely as part of their ignorance, of course."

The doctor's wife spoke one day with a woman in the ward, telling how wonderful it was that the Lord had healed her. To which the woman replied, "Ah, that poor one you worship. He has done what He could, but it was you people who did all the work. It was you who really healed me."

On another occasion, the doctor was about to perform a cataract operation.

As is their custom, he and his assistants first bowed their heads to pray for God's guidance, stating in the prayer that they depended upon the Lord to make the operation successful.

"Who is this Lord?" the patient protested. "I came to have Doctor Sahib fix my eyes. If Lord is going to do it, I'm going home!"

"Outright opposition, the lack of understanding on the part of the people, these are real problems," the doctor continued. "I wonder, though, if either of them is our greatest obstacle."

He looked up to me.

"I wonder, Ken, if our greatest problem has not been and continues to be a lack of real concern for the mission of the Church on the part of those who claim to be Christ's followers. Even out here, it is so easy to slip into complacency. Satan is a master craftsman. He cleverly inveigles us into being just busy enough in our Christian work to feel we are in God's will, but missing the real purposes God has for us. This is my daily concern, to break through the mere outer crust of activity one might call Christian and get to the real issues of our faith."

Now we both sat quietly.

I felt a stirring in my heart, as I looked at this man, and I thought of the others on the compound. Peter and Annette Warlow, Emmy, Monica, Miss Kunz. Others on the staff. I had seen them in strength. I had seen them in weakness. But, transcending any human observation, was the unmistakable evidence that each of them had made the kind of commitment which demands action.

What kind of commitment had I made?

And the multitudes of Christians back home, who had so much talent, so much they could give. If theirs was a greater commitment as individuals and as the mortal mosaic of the American Church, would the situation be different out here?

The doctor spoke of a lack of conviction among people in India? What about Christians back home? How sensitive were they to sin in their own lives? To wrong attitudes in the Church? To the reeking cancer of materialism affecting their lives in so many ways.

Might it be the Church was poised to detonate a final thrust of spiritual power across the world, sweeping multitudes into God's kingdom, but could not lest a spiritually insensitive Body commit blasphemy by keeping glory unto itself rather than ascribing all honor to the resurrected Christ?

The doctor longed, in his day, to see such a sweeping harvest. It was the ache of his heart.

Might it be that flames of compassion, ignited in my heart by my willingness for such to be, could somehow be the means of bringing the India dream into fuller realization?

29 Involvement.
A compassion for lost men.

I thought much about this, and how compassion and involvement had come into such obvious fruition at Herbertpur.

The more I thought about it, the more I realized stewardship must be the inevitable result of genuine compassion and involvement.

Partly out of timidity, I suppose, but also as

a matter of good taste, I had been reluctant to question the doctor as to his personal stewardship. If God has allowed any virtues to occur in my life, I would like to think one of them is a strong desire to respect the privacy of others.

Yet, the longer I stayed at Herbertpur and the better I got to know the doctor and his wife, the more clearly I saw stewardship in its fullest sense as the foundation to the entire Herbertpur story. To accurately recount this story, I must know much more of the doctor's stewardship attitudes. Resident in this man's attitude toward money, I was convinced, lay principles of dedication which ought to confront many Christians who, like myself, had so much to learn of what Christ meant when He said, *Lay not up for yourselves treasures on earth . . . but lay up for yourselves treasures in heaven.*

I had by this time been long enough at Herbertpur to realize once again the error of that religious sentimentality which places missionaries on a pedestal. The doctor is a man of great capacity for love and tenderness, but he is a man, and in moments of tension as the pressure of work mounted, the doctor and members of his staff at times behave very much like men.

"I have a tendency to be very stubborn," the doctor told me one day. "I constantly pray for victory over this. As I particularly look back on the early days of our ministry, I fear I was sometimes unfair with our workers. I expected too much of them."

To this day, the doctor's step continues to be brisk, his mind alert and versatile. The man who could have become a leader in English and Commonwealth industry does not content himself with mundane run-of-the-day projects. He likes action. Some, with a less virulent metabolism, tend to find him strong-willed and persistent. He is at times a target of criticism like any Christian leader who dares to take initiative.

The hospital staff works as a finely-organized team. They are like members of a common family, as is indeed the case in the fullest sense, but the work is hard and the hours long and it is inevitable for minds to grow weary and nerves to fray.

Human?

Yes.

But that is the majesty of it.

Unlike so many Christians, however, who have moments of spirituality, the doctor and his staff are best delineated as spiritual people who have moments of humanity.

My work has taken me to thirty and more of earth's mission fields, and has consequently planted my feet under many a missionary's table. I have listened to them share their problems. Often these are problems with other missionaries. The alarmingly high incidence of those who never come back for a second term stems, in numerous cases, from inadequate prior adjustments.

But I have learned something from observing missionaries.

The man who obviously could have succeeded in leadership back home invariably adjusts well on the mission field. This is a part of stewardship. The author of *African Queen* chose as one of his characters a deeply frustrated man who, when he realized he could never become a prominent clergyman, sought refuge in the Congo. There are missionaries like this. But a man, who has what it takes as the world says, and gives what he has to the harvest, is almost beyond exception a man who has involved himself in conscious, calculated dedication. He is a real philanthropist. God has endowed him with the capacity for success.

I knew Dr. Geoffrey D. Lehmann to be such a man.

It was not until autumn of 1964, however, when Dr. Lehmann came to America for final production work on the film and to spend several weeks in deputation, that I summoned courage to talk with him about the dedication of his personal stewardship to the Christian cause.

We had hidden away at a little cottage on Lake Michigan, devoting many hours to the further pursuit of the Herbertpur story. One afternoon, we took a relaxing walk along the beach, packed hard by the pounding surf of this beautiful, fresh water sea. The doctor delighted in the crisp mood of autumn.

"You need a touch of this during some of those hot days in India," I said.

He didn't answer, but I caught in his eye an expression I had noted in India. An unusually warm day, I remembered, and we had discussed the sweltering price paid by missionaries from the West who labor under the merciless Indian sun.

"There has always been in my mind the pull of worldliness," he had told me that day, "the desire to be someone important and well liked. Not only to have high educational degrees, but to have public recognition. This has perhaps made it easier for me to try to live a simple life of witness in this unknown jungle area, as a reaction to the known desire of my heart for public recognition."

Removed from the India setting, however, I had been relating him more to my own normal set of references. A man of warmth and wit and charm. A man of great skill. But a man, so quickly adapting himself to the plush contrast of his usual way of life, that it did not come natural for me to relate him to the steaming jungle.

That is, had it not been for that look in his eye as we walked along the beach.

"I enjoy getting back into the West like this," he said, as we paused now and looked out at the wide stretch of the water. "Really, though, it catches me rather out of my element."

At the moment, it seemed so very strange to hear him talk this way. Then I remembered.

We had arranged a number of speaking engagements for the doctor in our area, among them three college chapel addresses.

"I get terribly frightened at things like this, you know," the doctor had told us, "but I'll do whatever you say. I know you only want to help us make known the work at Herbertpur."

At first, my wife and I thought he was joking.

But he was really frightened. Again and again, as spellbound audiences listened to his quiet accounting of the India dream, there was plainly a tremor in his voice. So incredible, the dynamic, sure-voiced doctor at Herbertpur becoming the timid, hesitant, visitor to America.

But now I understood.

It was a totaling of the price he had paid to

wean himself from the pull of the flesh so that he might give himself in full commitment to the yearning of the spirit. In India, amidst the poverty and the heartache, he was strong and sure of himself. In America, with all of its call to materialistic ease, he could not permit himself to identify.

Many men condition themselves against spiritual perception. They think bank accounts and investments and capital gains, they think prestige and personal comfort, and it dulls their minds to the spirit. Beside me on the sand, however, stood a man who had insulated himself against the world, making it a stranger to him.

It was a kind of spiritual trauma. It stirred the heart to see.

"Doctor," I said, as we finished the steep climb back to the cottage, "the more I think about you and the Herbertpur story, the more I realize there is one basic characteristic, a first cause one might say, which needs to be accurately set forth, if that story is to make its fullest impact. People must see you and your unique commitment."

"I've got to watch you," he teased. "It's the Herbertpur story you want to tell, remember?"

"Without people," I reminded, "the hospital stood empty for a year, nothing more than dust and bricks, and without your commitment, there would never have been a Herbertpur story to tell."

We entered the cottage, and sat by the warm fireside.

"I believe the full story of your commitment can make a healing contribution to the wrong sense of values too many Christians have when it comes to stewardship," I continued.

"What do you mean?"

"Many Christians classify stewardship, and especially as it pertains to missions, as a kind of charity. To them, giving money is the final act. For example, a typical American Christian hears a message that stirs his heart. His impulse is to reach for his pocketbook. But he rarely thinks of giving himself."

"We realize, of course, that all Christians can't be in what we call full-time service," the doctor said.

"That is true," I agreed, "but every Christian owes it to himself and to God to be fully committed. I once heard it put this way. It's not how much of what we have we give to God, but how much of what belongs to God we keep for ourselves. As we have discussed before, money has a sacred essence, because it is the fruit of time and talents. A man's pocketbook cannot possibly be committed to God unless the man himself is committed to God. Stewardship . . . real stewardship . . . is a total experience.

"I have said that in order to say this. We can tell people about heathen darkness surrounding the hospital. We can tell them about the many who come for treatment. We can tell them about those who have professed faith in Christ, those who have suffered persecution because of their faith. The average Christian is conditioned to take all this in stride. He's heard it before and considers it commonplace. What the average Christian seldom faces, and does not want to face, is the basic motivation behind the hospital, the willingness of one man to commit both himself and his resources to God."

He sat quietly for a moment, studying the

252

fire.

"People have a natural awe for wealth," I continued. "The rich Christian, who gives his tithe and lives fat off of the remaining ninety percent, is usually considered to be quite a hero. Missions in America are supported by dollar bills, however, not by thousand dollar checks."

"It's a similar circumstance in England."

"I realize your natural compulsion to keep your financial matters to yourself, Dr. Lehmann. I think this is right. But the principles which govern your stewardship, in my opinion, ought to be out for clear view."

"I am naturally quite reluctant to talk about it," he said, selecting his words with deliberation. "I have also learned to respect the counsel and the convictions of those who share my concern for Christians who do not understand that God only bestows his choicest blessings upon those who seek to withhold nothing from Him."

He grew quiet again, deeply contemplative. He stepped to the fire and stirred the logs on the grate, and they caught full flame. It seemed this was his full interest, the glowing hearth, but by now I knew him too well to believe it. I knew too much of the hungers in his heart.

"Perhaps my stewardship is not so unusual as you might think," he said at last. "In a sense, it was made possible by the personal convictions of my parents. As you know, the Bible says, *train up a Child in the way he should go, and when he is old, he will not depart from it.*"

"Your parents thought of economic blessings in terms of spiritual responsibility?"

"Very much so. We were given all we needed as children. All we needed and much more, as is so often the case with parents who are devoted to their children. But we were never allowed to be extravagant. My father found real joy in giving liberally to many phases of the Lord's work, and from my earliest childhood, I was taught the joy of giving. Not just the tithe, but much more than that."

Hesitant at first, he spoke more and more freely as our conversation continued. He chose his remarks with propriety, but I sensed a note of new discovery in his voice, the joy of finding an unanticipated avenue for molding the hearts of others who might thereby share with him the vision of a world and its need.

"Even though my economic situation is unusual," he said with intense feeling, "I am a missionary because I am a man with a mission to perform for the Lord Jesus Christ. It was He who commanded His followers to go into all the world and preach the Gospel. In the matter of economics, I am sure few people realize that the position of a missionary with his own financial backing has its special problems, because such a missionary must watch his spending as a true steward of the Lord. Some missionaries are controlled in what they can or cannot spend by the fact that God sends them, or withholds from them, funds for their work. In our case, we have continually made it a matter of much prayer for God's guidance as to how we should use the income from our personal investments. There have been times when, in ourselves, we felt like moving into certain projects. We had the money to do so. But, in answer to prayer, we have felt definitely directed by the

Holy Spirit not to move ahead. It has been thrilling to see, again and again, how time has vindicated these decisions."

I knew, from previous observation, how strongly he feels about the wise utilization of both time and money. He takes great care to make sure all purchasing is done wisely. This alone has saved the hospital thousands of dollars. Though he refrains from divulging specific information, I found many reasons to suspect that, brick for brick and patient for patient, no missionary hospital anywhere in the world operates more economically than does Herbertpur.

"When Monica and I first came to India," he told me, "we didn't have the money we have now since my father's death, and since my wife came into her own inheritance. We had to face up to the fact that we were starting a work which could move only as the Lord supplied the need. Many times I would go to my knees, deeply concerned lest we were going ahead more quickly than we could carry the load. It was only later, after we had built the hospital, that our financial position enabled us to carry on without worrying about it.

"When we first came to India, the money we both had was all we had. No one backed us financially. We were on the prayer list of the Brethren, but with our name in italics, indicating we did not need personal support. From this, people got the idea we needed no help for the work, either, and thus through the years there has not been regular support. By far the major cost of the hospital has had to be borne by ourselves."

In those early years, the young couple was not without an occasional taste of the blessing of special provision, however. Gifts did come from people in England, invariably in times of special needs. The doctor's father, too, sent financial aid.

Gifts still come to the hospital, most of them earmarked for the Poor Patients' Fund. While he was in the United States, the doctor set up a North American office for the purpose of handling special contributions to the work.

The doctor has his capital diversified three ways.

"I have what I call my own personal money," he told me, "and secondly the trust I have made for my children, and then the trusts I have made for charitable work."

Most of his own personal funds have been invested in England, as well as in the United States, providing livelihood for the Lehmanns in addition to profits which the doctor transfers to his charitable trust.

"I have set a ceiling for my own personal worth," he said. "As soon as my money reaches this point, I transfer all excess to the charitable trust. This trust is operated by a board of directors, the same as a non-profit corporation in the United States, and funds from these trusts finance Herbertpur Hospital, the publication of books and tracts for distribution in India, as well as other special projects."

While the doctor has crossed the bridge of committed stewardship, and has neither reason nor inclination to turn back, he enjoys the role of the financier. He has no personal profit motive, to be sure, but the desire to provide funds for a growing ministry keep him on constant alert for good investment opportunities.

256

Several years ago, by way of example, the rapid increase of ministry opportunities at Herbertpur sent costs spiraling. The pace of increased fiscal requirements began to give the doctor cause for concern. He saw the need to make a shift in investments, which would provide a substantial increase in annual dividend returns.

He decided to approach Lloyds of London, the world's foremost insurance firm, to investigate the possibitiy of becoming one of the coveted "Names at Lloyds," as the organization's underwriters are called.

Lloyds is a prestige firm. To become a name at Lloyds, a man must not only have a sizeable financial statement, but he must be every inch an English gentleman. Consequently, an intensive study is made of each applicant. If the study warrants, the applicant is given an interview with the president. Final approval rests in the hands of the executive board.

"There was some question as to whether or not they would accept anyone not living in England," the doctor said, "and so it was a thrilling surprise when I learned they were willing to take me as the only non-resident member."

During the inital months, the fortunes of Lloyds gave the doctor considerable concern, so much so that he seriously wondered if he had made a wise move. Through the ensuing years, however, the wisdom of the decision has been substantially validated.

It is of at least passing interest that names at Lloyds are divided into groups and listed alphabetically. In one such group, directly below the name Geoffrey D. Lehmann, one finds Harold B. Macmillan.

A London attorney serves as liasion. The doctor, who keeps careful watch on investment trends through a study of periodicals airmailed from England, renders his decisions by cable.

I asked, "What is your attitude toward speculation on the stock market?"

"Are you speaking in terms of speculation whereby one buys stock, without paying for it, on the speculation that it will increase or decrease by the end of the month when payment shall be made?"

"That's one aspect."

"I believe this is completely wrong. Gambling in any form, even in the guise of business procedure, is improper Christian conduct. On the other hand, however, looking into the condition of a firm, determining what sort of men serve as the directors, examining statistics on the company's progress, and then deciding to make an investment in that firm because one feels it has good possibilities is, I believe, a marvelous way of handling the money given us with which we are to be stewards."

"Then you are interested mainly in long-term investments?"

"Decidedly so. If I have stock in a company, which after a period of a year or so does not appear to be doing well, and if another firm appears to be more promising, naturally I sell my stock in the one company and reinvest in the other."

"But you are mainly interested in obtaining earnings from your investments, not from purchasing stock at one price and selling at another."

"I am completely opposed to that type of

speculation," he said firmly. "I would no more play the stock market, as you Americans call it, than I would buy a lottery ticket or place a bet at a horse race!"

Continued discussion with the doctor showed clearly his pattern of thinking. To him, the words investment and stewardship share a common nomenclature.

Back at Herbertpur, he is often seen strolling in the garden, or in quiet meditation on the back veranda, as the song of the bird he so dearly loves, the kastura, heralds the first glow of morning. During these moments, he is not Geoffrey Lehmann, the man of medicine, but Geoffrey Lehmann, the businessman, reviewing in his mind each facet of his fiscal enterprise. He not only seeks divine guidance upon every decision, but bathes each continuing investment with faithful intercession.

This kind of spiritual scrutiny engulfs the full gamut of his life, from source of supply to the tools for the harvest.

He loves to talk about hospital equipment, the care given to study and purchase of each item. Close to his heart lies the literature ministry made possible by his initial investment, sustained by returns from sales and his continuing stewardship.

His eyes glow at the mention of ministry among the Tibetans. For years, occasional merchants trekking the trade routes between Lhasa and New Delhi, as well as lamas on pilgrimages to Buddhist shrines in India, made occasional visits to the hospital. Each received a copy of the Tibetan scriptures, to read and to bring back beyond the Himalayas. Now, with thousands of refugees driven out of Tibet and into India, making possible evangelistic opportunities for which they have prayed so long, he keeps a close watch for ministry opportunities. The Tibetan students of Wynberg-Allen Schools are close to his heart, and only the temporal demands of the hospital's ministry prevent him from closer work and contact with them.

"Do you believe stewardship is the key to prosperity?" I asked. It was a question I had wanted to pose for some time.

"Well," he replied, "the Bible tells us God loves the cheerful giver. In Malachi, He promises to open the windows of heaven upon those who give. *The liberal soul shall be made fat,* Solomon wrote. But it's not a matter of manipulating God's goodness. God looks at our hearts, at our motives. *Lay not up for yourselves treasures upon earth,* the Lord Jesus told us, *but lay up for yourselves treasures in heaven.* For some Christians, affluence is like poison. If they sincerely sought God's best, it might be necessary for Him to answer their prayers by taking their possessions from them."

"Wealth then is relative?" I asked.

"Most certainly, Ken. Stewardship begins first in the heart. The widow's mite was all she had, and it was exceedingly precious in the Savior's eyes!"

The heart.

The inner man.

I prayed that God would never let me forget it, that He would purify my motives and, somehow, let me convey to others the gripping inspiration of these hours.

In looking through published accounts of the Herbertpur ministry, supplied by the doctor for my research, I came upon a prayer he wrote some years ago, as he sought to put into writing the compulsions deep in his heart.

Oh my God, possess my soul with such a fervent love of Thee that it may transcend all earthly loves. Bring my whole being into such a deep fellowship with Thee that Thy love may flow through me to permeate all around, filling those I meet with Thy joy which none can take away. That my touch may be Thee in me, so that in the daily affairs of life it will be as gentle and tender, yet as firm and strong as was Thine in Christ Jesus. That Thy peace, the peace of Thy presence that passeth all understanding, may flow through me as Thy river, the River of Life, will flow from Thy throne to the healing of the nations.

Give to the Church more men who pray like that! Men with strong hands and dedicated minds and tender hearts! Men who dare to cry out from their hearts and vividly demonstrate through their lives the dedication of the apostle who wrote, *But what things were gain to me, those I counted loss for Christ. Yea, doubtless, I count all things but loss for the excellency of the knowledge of Christ Jesus my Lord: for whom I have suffered the loss of all things, and do count them but dung that I may win Christ . . . that I may know Him, and the power of His resurrection, and the fellowship of His suffering, being made conformable unto His death.*

30 Several years ago, enroute to a committee meeting at Wynberg-Allen Schools, Dr. Lehmann stopped for gas in

Dehra Dun. As he drove away, he heard a mechanical noise, pulled in to investigate, discovered one of the brakes had developed a slight malfunction. It would take an hour to repair, and since he was on a tight schedule, he left the Land Rover and hired a private car.

Late that evening, returning from Mussoorie, he picked up the repaired vehicle and drove back to the Hospital.

"The next morning," he says, "Monica and I, together with two others, started off once again to Dehra Dun. We had gone about five miles on the Dehra road, when a lorry was standing on my side of the highway. I veered to pass it, and went by without difficulty, but when I again turned the wheel to get back onto the road, nothing happened. Instead, we plunged into a slanting twelve-foot ditch, rolling onto our side, all of us together in a heap. The steering gear had broken."

People came running from all directions, more than one shouting in panic, "Doctor Sahib is killed!"

But the doctor and his party were all unhurt, though badly shaken.

As he crawled out of the automobile and examined the situation, Dr. Lehmann did a quick bit of mental arithmetic. Had it not been for the odd mechanical noise, which caused him to change cars in Dehra Dun, this would have happened near the bottom of the mountain. Each year, several vehicles careen off the road and plunge down the dizzying embankments.

Rarely does a driver or his riders live to tell what happened.

"This was the second time that, in a most remarkable way, the Lord saved my life," he relates. "During the war, I had booked passage on a train but, at the last moment, found it necessary to change my plans. The train was wrecked, and on the particular car where I would have ridden, all passengers lost their lives."

God has not only spared his life, but has kept him in consistent health through the years. Those years have passed quickly, and their passing gives much cause for reminiscence.

There is also need to think of the future.

"I must soon make plans for retirement," the doctor told me. "Yet we simply have no one at the moment to look to for replacement. This is the way it has been all these years. When Peter goes on furlough, I shall be sixty-two, and must once again bear the full burden of the work. Our hearts cry out to God for help. There is such wonderful opportunity here."

He has no thought of leaving India, however. None at all. Perhaps the two of them will spend six months in England, six months on the field. Like Emmy, they will invest the whole of their years in the harvest.

"When my eyesight will no longer permit delicate surgery, I would like to give more time to literature evangelism. With the closing of the schools, this became my second interest. Perhaps it shall one day be my first."

But this is not all.

These many years, he has felt the deep hurt of the poverty so prevalent in the area. The fields are small and must be divided again and again among sons and grandsons. There is no crop rotation.

One day he stopped at a government research station, and saw a chart showing the many different crops which could be grown in the Herbertpur area. Listed among them was menthol, a potential cash crop which, if successfully grown, could raise land value substantially. It was decided to experiment.

While in India, I examined the test plot at the hospital compound, and saw tangible reason for the doctor's pleasure. His first menthol crop was harvested and sent to the research center. The report is that it produced a good grade of oil.

"If the experiment proves successful, and we feel quite sure it is going to be," the doctor told me, "we hope to build a small distillery, so we can draw the oil right here. It is possible for our farmers to realize a cash return ten to fifteen times greater than what they get from rice and wheat."

Physical poverty, intense though it may be, gives precedence in the doctor's concern to spiritual poverty. When he and his beloved Monica first came to Herbertpur, they dreamed of an indigenous church, a central meeting place serving villages even as the hospital provides medical aid to a large area.

No such church has come into being.

"God has taught us a wonderful lesson through this disappointment," the doctor says. "We realize, what every Christian should clearly understand, that the Church is not a building or even a given group of people as such. The Church is individuals, whether one individual or a hundred, so long as each individual has come to a personal knowledge of God through Jesus Christ."

In this sense, the Church has come to the Jamuna valley. It has come to the little mother hovering over her cooking pots, and quietly humming a song of redemption heard at the Hospital and experienced in her heart. It has come to the farmer in his field, who sees his brother at work nearby and well knows the animosity in his kinsmens' hearts, but thanks *Yesu Masih* for the presence of God in his own life. It has come to little children, who have listened to Emmy and Mrs. Mall at the hospital, and have snatched the first understanding of the song *Jesus Loves Me*.

Yet, looking to the future, the doctor and his co-laborers envision organized bodies of believers. This still lies central to the India dream, and there is now a ray of hope. The Indian government is developing an enormous hydro-electric plant on the Jamuna River, only a short drive from the hospital. The scheme is to bring industry to the valley.

"Perhaps then our established church will come," the doctor says. A deep yearning mellows his voise. "Perhaps Christians will come in from the south, where there are thousands of believers, and they will be an encouragement to our scattered Christians here. Together they could build a church, and thus bring to glorious fruition the many years of spiritual planting and watering."

Meanwhile, the doctor's main concern continues to be planting and watering, and gathering the gleaner's harvest from among those who hear and hearing begin to hunger.

"So many wait to hear, and even among those who have come to the hospital, and who have heard something of the Lord, there is so much to be done."

The doctor illustrates his point by telling of a man contacted by one of the workers, who asked if he knew of Jesus.

"Yes," the man said, "but He is dead."

"Dead?" the worker asked, taken completely by surprise. "Why do you say that?"

"I bought a book about Him," the man said. It was one of the Gospels. "I read of Jesus, and my heart was filled with hope. I read of His love and His many miracles. Then I read how they took Him and crucified Him and He died. I was so discouraged, I put the book away."

"But you should have read on!" the hospital worker said. "It is true Jesus died. He died for our sins. But He rose again, triumphant over death."

Together, they opened the Bible and read the account of the resurrection, and the man went away rejoicing in the reality of the risen Christ!

The India dream.

It is a figment of eternity.

It is long years and much toil, careful planting and watering and the slow, slow gathering of the harvest. But there is harvest and, though the modest doctor wisely gives God the glory of all accomplishments, the fact remains that God uses men. He has used Doctor Sahib these years at Herbertpur.

Never more poignantly has this been documented than the day one of the workers went into a village selling literature. There he met an old man who had first heard the Gospel and believed some twenty-five years earlier, when the hospital was new.

"Doctor Sahib told me about Jesus," the old man said. "It was when he first came, many years ago. I am not a learned man, but I have seen Christ in the life of the doctor, and because of this I have believed. The doctor is like Jesus. Jesus came from heaven to save us, and the doctor came all the way from England to tell us about it!"

Yes, the doctor came all the way from England. He was young then, and the India dream glowed in his heart. He was one of the few who heard the call to action and obeyed.

Thus there is light at Herbertpur, light in the hearts of those who have believed, light for those who seek.

But across India, and across the world, there are many more potential Herbertpurs. They lie untouched, barren spiritual wastelands, because other young engineers and teachers and doctors and farmers and multitudes more likewise heard the call but did not heed.

Through all his years of ministry, no other burden has rested more heavily upon Doctor Sahib's heart!

Saturday the 17th, September 1983.

The date marked eighteen years and two months since the publication of this book.

But much more.

For on that date, Geoffrey and Monica Lehmann celebrated the fiftieth year of their marriage.

In observing the metamorphosis of ministries, someone once said, "First there is the man, then the movement, then a monument."

Geoffrey Lehmann not only wanted this never to be the case with him, but undertook painful procedures necessary to avoid such ministry fossilization.

During more than four decades of outreach among the Himalayan foothills, Dr. Sahib, as he came to be affectionately known, was both pivot and periphery to the Herbertpur ministry.

"At times," he relates, "Monica and I all but despaired, so desperate was our need for competent help, so futile our efforts searching for those who could assist us."

Often, when circumstances necessitated the doctor being away, he had no recourse but to furlough the hospital except for what limited facility the nursing staff could provide.

"Many times I wondered if our ministry had a future. The years sped by so quickly. Although I have enjoyed abundant health, I knew I could not continue indefinitely."

Yet, though he seemingly searched in vain for those into whose hands he could entrust the hospital, Dr. Sahib knew, deep in his heart, that Solomon's God had a plan and would reveal this plan at the appointed and appropriate time. *(Ecclesiastes 3:1)*

It was a confidence spawned from many years' searching of the Scriptures, searching and believing.

Geoffrey Lehmann reached the age of normal retirement. Yet the work continued to grow, demands upon his time unrelenting, the search for a "Timothy" to assume responsibility unrewarded.

He had to be increasingly meticulous with eye operations, his own sight yielding to the debilitation of so many passing years.

Even so, on his seventieth birthday he conducted an eye camp in a mountain village and that day performed one hundred operations!

Evangelism comes one-by-one at best in the Herbertpur environs. Yet, again and again, fruit resulted from the ministry of love, the sowing of spiritual seed.

This book abounds with examples. Here are a few of the many more since the closing of those initial pages.

****

At one of the hospital's Sunday afternoon Gospel services, news spread among patients and relatives that something strange was about to happen. Consequently, a much larger than usual group assembled. Suddenly, a TB patient strode onto the platform.

Courage glistened in his eyes, determination quickened his step, denying evidence of the tension searing like a fire inside him.

Pulling his choti *(the long lock of hair all orthodox Hindus proudly display)*, he cut it off, saying, "This is to show you all that I have become a Christian. Jesus Christ is my Savior!"

A few months earlier, like a skin-covered skeleton, this man had crawled into the hospital courtyard, awaiting the moment when he would gasp his final breath.

Dr. Lehmann's diagnosis was pulmonary tuberculosis in its terminal stage.

But medicine and loving care stayed the hand of death. During the months of convalescence, he heard, day after day, the wonderful story of salvation.

He was a man who had known much of human anguish and, as he regained health, told the Lehmanns his story.

During the time of the partition of India, he and his highest caste Brahmin family lived in a little Punjab village. One day the village was attacked by a screaming hoard of Muslims who, having fired the thatched roofs, waited for residents to rush out so they could be cut down and killed.

Fortunately, this man's house stood at the back of the village, near the forest, enabling him and his sister to escape before their enemies could reach them. Every moment held the specter of imminent terror.

At last, they reached a station where a train was just starting off — filled with Hindu refugees fleeing, or so they thought, to safety.

The train had gone but a short distance, however, when the engineer closed the throttle. In horror, passengers looked out to see the tracks ahead covered by multitudes of Muslims, defying the engineer to run over them.

As the train braked to a stop, bands of shouting men stormed aboard and began massacring the Hindus.

This man's sister was killed but he managed to escape through a window and, after several terrifying months of wandering, reached the hospital — to be cured of his disease and to know the Lord Jesus as his Savior!

****

From the earliest Herbertpur beginnings, Monica and Geoffrey had prayed to see little churches raised up in the villages. It seemed impossible, so deep ran the undercurrents of unbelief and prejudice. It has taken years of patience, years of faithfully demonstrating the power of God and the authenticity of the Gospel. Now, slowly but steadily, a few small congregations are taking root in this Himalayan area.

For God has been at work, blessing His Word, touching hearts.

The Lehmanns have a staunchly Bible-based mode of ministry. They realize how some look askance at such phenomena as dreams.

"It has been a discipline for us to learn," Geoffrey says, "that among people who have absolutely no means of hearing the Gospel, but sincerely seek to know the truth, our Lord often resorts to Old Testament methods to awaken and guide those who seek."

A man whose whole body was so riddled with tuberculosis that there seemed no possibility of curing him was lovingly attended at Herbertpur by his wife and young children. During this time they trusted in the Lord but somehow he could not get real peace of heart, until one night the Lord appeared to him in a dream and spoke to him saying, "Why are you worrying in this way? You have trusted in me and I who died to save you, will, you can be sure, take you to be with me when you die and I will look after your family."

It was wonderful to see this man the next morning with *the peace of God which passeth all understanding* written all over his face!

But it is the solid, steady ministry of the Word of God which has made the substantial difference. This was illustrated at an eye camp one day when, prior to beginning surgery, Geoffrey took time, as he always did, to present the Gospel to awaiting patients.

In this case Muslims.

When the Lehmanns first brought the Gospel into the hills, they had to use utmost discretion. Followers of Islam see rejection of the Gospel and persecution of Christians as a noble act for those who live by the Koran.

Yet on this occasion, as one Dr. Geoffrey Lehmann, like Peter of old, boldly proclaimed, *"Neither is there salvation in any other; for there is no other name under heaven given among men, whereby we must be saved,"* the crowd listened in rapt courtesy.

Suddenly, one of the village elders leaped to his feet. Perhaps he was a *haji*, one who has made the pilgrimage to Mecca. In the past, his bent would have been to rebuke the doctor and bid him to be silent.

Instead, and in a voice resonant with conviction, the old man said, "Yes, that's quite right what the Doctor Sahib is saying! Jesus is the Son of God! He is our Savior! I have trusted Him since I and my wife heard about Him at Herbertpur many years ago."

Lucid and dauntless proclamation of the

Word of God itself has always been central to Monica's and Geoffrey's evangelistic outreach. But also contributing to the success of their efforts has been the special embellishments the doctor often gives to message presentation.

For example.

"You really don't need us here, do you?" he would sometimes say, introducing an evangelistic homily given prior to mobile clinic eye surgeries.

Villagers would mumble among themselves, then call out. "But, Doctor Sahib, we do need you!"

"Why do you need me?" the doctor would tease. "Can you not find a spoon here in your village, and use it to take the bad cataracts from your eyes?"

Laughter would ensue, with happy cries of, "No! No! Only your hands have the skill to give us our sight! We cannot do it ourselves!"

"Neither can you cleanse your hearts of sin," the doctor then would continue, as a hush fell upon his hearers. "Some of you have tried. You think by good works you can take away your sins. But the Bible tells us *Christ died for our sins.* It also tells us *Whosoever shall call upon the name of the Lord shall be saved.*"

One here, two there, in village after village across the hills, blind hearts have called and had the cataracts of sin and disbelief removed!

Yet, of the ninety million inhabitants in the State of Uttar Pradesh, only one percent are even nominal Christians.

The work has only just begun.

In contrast to sparce spiritual harvesting in

the north, South India has a large Christian population. Discrimination runs strong between North and South. Even so, obedient to their Lord's call, many southern Christians come north as missionaries, pastors and evangelists.

One such man was Emmanuel Raj. An electronics engineer for Indian Railways, the young man had a bright future.

But a restless and empty heart.

Someone gave him a copy of Oswald Smith's book *The Spirit at Work*. Reading it, the young man saw his need for personal transformation and was converted.

He left his position, spent five years in further training, preparing himself for Christian service.

Then someone told him about Herbertpur.

Emmanuel Raj applied, and the Lehmanns readily employed him.

Acceptance of the South Indian and his talented wife was slow at first. When I was doing research on the chapters of this book, a North Indian businessman told me, "He is an absolutely stupid fellow. He's hopeless. He should be sent back to the South. But Dr. Lehmann is such a soft-hearted chap, he will likely let him stay."

Stay the Rajs did.

And, through their persistent effort, the Word of God began to penetrate into the community. Today, just a five–minute drive from the Lehmanns' present residence, a large chapel stands. Not a dozen, not forty or fifty, but on Sundays up to two hundred attend worship! In one recent year, eighty new converts were baptised!

It could never have happened when the

Lehmanns first arrived in Herbertpur.

The little chapel at Rajpur has become a token of God's faithfulness. As detailed in the earlier pages of this book, they knew God called them to India, to the unevangelized hills above Herbertpur and Rajpur. Through years of discouragement, when they seemed to go unrewarded in their efforts to establish an outreach ministry beyond the hospital, God gave them continuing assurance that His Word would not return void. Rajpur, and the few little chapels here and there in the villages, stand in living attestation!

One of the chapel's senior elders, now a bank accountant, was born and reared in a mountain village. How he came to his present state offers yet another facet illustrating the faithfulness of God and the authority of His Word.

Chatunki, his older sister, fell prey to the relentless plague of the hills, tuberculosis. She came to the hospital and spent six months in the TB block.

It is the TB therapy which has been the most fruitful in the evangelistic ministry of the hospital, patients remaining for long periods of time and thus coming under the continued influence of the Gospel.

But Chatunki, having a mind and will of her own, resisted the Gospel message. Yet, though she withstood the Holy Spirit's pleading, she could not insulate her mind and heart against the Scriptures.

Returning to her mountain village, she told her family about the Lord Jesus.

Keenly interested, her brother, on one of his journeys to the lowlands, purchased a New Testament. He read it avidly, shared its contents with other members of the family.

Chatunki also listened, recognizing many of the Scriptures she had heard at the hospital.

But she continued to resist.

One day the brother announced to his household that, through reading the New Testament, he had become a Christian. The transformation in his life caused the other eight members of his family to give closer heed, and subsequently all were baptised.

At last, through the patient witness of her brother and other members of her family, whom she herself had introduced to the Gospel, Chatunki also believed and was baptised!

Even as the harvest of hearts began to turn golden, so the Sovereign Lord rewarded the prayers of faith for the hospital's future.

There had been a Dr. Warlow, a physician and surgeon of skill whose first motivation was always a patient's spiritual need.

"Both Monica and I saw him as the one who would take over the work." Geoffrey remembers. "He got along so well with the people, had a good grasp of the language, but family needs necessitated his return to England.

"It was a great blow to us."

Yet the Lehmanns' faith did not waver. God had led them to India. God had blessed their decades of effort. Agencies like Christian Blind Mission International had funded projects with long-term outreach potential. The Great Physician would not let the ministry die.

Christian hospitals dot the face of India. The competent and unselfish service offered by these benevolent institutions has done much to enhance the Christian image across the land.

Also in the North, in a goverment hospital, worked Dr. Ray Windsor as an associate professor of heart surgery. He and his wife are longtime friends of the Lehmanns and visited the hospital regularly to do major surgery. It was during this time that he, together with Geoffrey and a number of other leaders, envisaged a national organization (Emmanuel Hospital Association) which would bind evangelical Christian hospitals together in a unity of function and purpose.

About this time Geoffrey was taking part in a Sunday morning service when he noticed a stranger seated at the back of the hall. Geoffrey went to him and asked him to join the small group of worshipers. As they chatted, Geoffrey learned that the visitor was Dr. Cy Satow, a Japanese-American in charge of a Christian hospital on the Indo-Pakistan border for many years. He had heard of the need at Herbertpur and sensed the Lord calling him there!

A few months later, Cy Satow became the new Medical Superintendent at Herbertpur; the answer to long years of persistent prayer. Dr. Paul Phuntsog, an orthopedic specialist, joined a few months later and then Susanna, the Lehmanns' youngest daughter, with her husband Paul East, became part of the hospital staff. Paul is the hospital administrator and coordinator for EHA administrative training.

The hospital has changed. The folksiness engendered by the Lehmanns, the evenings spent with groups of patients lying in open sheds when sufficient wards were not available, singing Christian hymns set to mountain folk tunes and teaching them verses from the Bible — these days are now gone.

But the spiritual outreach remains strong, as vital and consistent as when the Lehmanns were in charge.

Lingering disappointment came to Geoffrey during a discussion with an old and trusted friend when he asked if he and Monica should remain at the hospital to devote their golden years to ministry among the patients. No, they were told, it would not be good for the founder to live on the premises. He should select a place of residence some distance away but could visit weekly, which they do.

It pleases Geoffrey that Dr. Satow and his associates exercise the same priorities the founders had and are able to give even better medical care.

Their first objective is the same that brought the Lehmanns to India, using medicine as a means of opening heart doors to the Gospel. They just do it in a slightly different way.

Today, Doctor Sahib's most prominent role on behalf of the hospital is the development of what he calls the Poor Patients' Fund. Expedient property purchases have enabled him to establish long term sources of income.

Most exciting and rewarding, however, is a new outreach.

Writing.

"I never thought of myself as a writer," Geoffrey says, "don't necessarily do so now. But my mind is full of ideas."

Lyrics, a book of competent verse, was published several years ago. More recently, he has written four books in a series of adventure stories for children. Built around one "Asha," the lead character, these books are slanted primarily toward Indian youth but an American publisher has taken the rights to release to a world-wide audience. Also, a series of six books, *The Secret Sign* series, have been accepted for publication.

All earnings will go into the Poor Patients' Fund and for printing evangelical tracts and booklets.

My own continuing associations with Geoffrey have involved his participation in the production of several motion pictures.

Tashi from Tibet resulted from our initial meeting. The film visualized the plight of Tibetans fleeing from their mountain kingdom.

Next came *Jouney to the Sky*, a motion picture based on the amazing life of Sadhu Sundar Singh. Now translated into many languages, this film is involved in consistent outreach across the Third World.

The most spiritually productive release has been *Yoneko*, a true story of a Japanese teenager who attempted suicide by jumping in front of a train. In Japan and elsewhere, *Yoneko* has become a vital tool in the harvesting of young hearts.

As this is written, Geoffrey is involved in plans for filming a children's adventure story in England.

He has also been partially involved in the production of at least a dozen other Christian films and has established procedures for continuing involvement.

Monica and Geoffrey now spend approximately eight months of the year in their beloved India, four months at their lovely home in Shoreham, Kent, just a half-hour by train south of London.

Though an octogenarian, the doctor walks with a sprightly step, has the speech and manner of a man driven by purpose and persistently in a hurry.

Time has passed relentlessly until now. Time will continue it's rapid flight. But Geoffrey Lehmann–beloved Doctor Sahib–lives by the conviction that one's alloted time on earth is strategic to one's unending status in eternity.

Much too fulfilled to count the years and much too busy to grow old, he determines to live by his Lord's promise, *the man who does the will of God lives forever!*

****

EPILOGUE

The science of medicine depends upon experimentation for its development. Thus the term "guinea pig" has come to be a part of the medical world's nomenclature.

In a sense, this book is about a "guinea pig," although it might be more accurate to speak of what happened as a demonstration rather than as an experiment. In any case, this book is the report of what happened to a man, showing the divine treatment given and the results obtained. My prayer is that others may benefit from the spiritaul knowledge thus obtained.

In 1963, while in northern India making plans for the film TASHI FROM TIBET, Ken Anderson mentioned that he might like to write a book about my life and our work at Herbertpur which, for various reasons, he considered rather unusual. He felt that such a book might possibly be of help to others in similar circumstances.

At the time, I did not take Mr. Anderson seriously. However, from time to time we discussed the matter and, later, having read our circular letters and the two pamphlets I had written about the work at Herbertpur, he asked me to answer some questions on the tape recorder.

Knowing how badly I speak extemporarily, I rather dared myself to do this, feeling sure the result would be such that Mr. Anderson would drop the matter.

But, somehow, as we went ahead with the interview, he felt the Herbertpur story contained material which could be presented for the Lord's glory, and so we proceeded. Our plan was for him to rough out an initial draft of the manuscript, and we would then subsequently get together and edit out any errors as well as portions which to my mind might seem a bit egotistical.

Then came a letter telling of the opportunity extended by WORLD BOOKS to have the manuscript puslished as a part of their initial programm. This would necessitate my waiving the discussion sessions we had planned, and which we both thought important.

After much prayer, I felt it wise to accept the WORLD BOOKS offer. But there was one agreement we must make. Mr. Anderson would concentrate on what the Lord Jesus Christ had done, the book would show how He could use weakness and failure, the emphasis would be on how He had sustained me by His matchless grace.

Not I, but Christ!

GEOFFREY D. LEHMANN M.D.
Herbertpur Christian Hospital
Dist. Dehra Dun, (U.P.) India

P.S. (1985)

I am glad this book is being re-published by the Christian Blind Mission International, (a division of Christoffel-Blindenmission, West Germany) which has been wholeheartedly supporting the ministry of Herbertpur Christian Hospital for many years now, and for which I am deeply grateful to God.

HIMALAYAN HEARTBEAT

By KEN ANDERSON . . .

The stirring story of Christianity in action in India. A penetrating portrait of a Christian surgeon who exchanged a brilliant business career to help the people of the Himalayan foothills.

This is a true story, reported in first person by the author. Ken Anderson was there. He met Dr. Geoffrey D. Lehmann and his wife. He met the patients at Herbertpur Hospital. He watched the doctor operate. He learned, as he gained the confidence of the Lehmanns, something of their astonishing background . . . that Geoffrey Lehmann is a graduate engineer . . . that he inherited the familiy business in England . . . that on the brink of what promised to be an outstanding career in business came the decision to prepare for a life as a missionary medic to the people of India. He discovered that Dr. Lehmann is the only non-resident of England to be one of the "Names" (underwriters) at Lloyds of London.

Most important, Ken Anderson learned the "why" of all this, and reveals the answer in the dramatic unfolding of the events that provide the setting and situation of HIMALAYAN HEARTBEAT.

Ken Anderson and his wife, Doris, have enjoyed a close friendship with Dr. and Mrs. Geoffrey Lehmann for many years. They have visited the Lehmanns in India and hosted them at their home in America.

The Andersons founded Ken Anderson Films more than a quarter century ago and have produced audio-visuals in many parts of the world. These include several films in association with the Lehmanns.

Two of the best known motion pictures produced overseas are PILGRIMS PROGRESS, filmed in Great Britain, and SOME THROUGH THE FIRE, the documentation of Christians in Uganda during the years of persecution.

North American releases include FANNY CROSBY, HUDSON TAYLOR, SECOND STEP and a four-part seminar on personal witness.

As a free-lance writer, Mr. Anderson has published many books and is a frequent contributor to numerous magazines. In 1962 he was named Magazine Feature Writer of the Year by Evangelical Press Association.

He travels three times annually to Singapore to conduct sessions in audio visuals at the Haggai Institute, a short-term training program for credentialed Third World nationals. Because of his extensive work throughout what wasthe British Empire, he is included in *Men of Achievement*, published by the International Biographical Centre of Cambridge, England. His biography also appears in *Who's Who in the United States* and *Who's Who in the Midwest*.

APPENDIX

I

CBMI Beneficiaries

Today — the very day you are reading this — CBMI's ministry will

provide for	19,868	blind people
teach	8,080	deaf-mute students
rehabilitate	6,337	physically handi-capped people
educate	5,019	mentally disabled people
train	1,950	multi-handicapped people
nurse	307	elderly people
mother	438	orphans
give medicine to	8,097	destitute and penniless people
restore sight to	379	blind people
save sight of	293	sight-endangered people
give glasses to	747	people with visual handicaps
care for	309	leprosy patients
give therapy to	67	crippled people fitted with artificial limbs
treat	73	tuberculosis patients
feed and help	120,000	malnourished people and disaster victims
preach the Gospel to	171,964	needy people eager to hear more about God's Love.

CBMI-Projects

In 96 countries, the community of CBMI friends and supporters maintains:

120	Boarding Schools for the Blind
6	Braille Printing Presses
62	Workshops for the Blind
38	Training Farms for the Blind
9	Radio and Cassette Ministries
11	Bible Schools and Teacher Training Colleges
67	Schools for the Deaf
107	Centres for the Disabled
42	Homes for the Multi-Handicapped
15	Orphanages
11	Nursing Homes for the Aged
9	Feeding Centres
3	Well Drilling Teams
59	Social Welfare Centres
103	Dispensaries
22	Mobile Clinics
5	Flying Eye Doctors' Services
241	Eye Hospitals
43	Optical Workshops
26	Leprosy Clinics
4	Leprosy Hospitals
27	Orthopaedic Clinics
20	T.B. Treatment Centres
108	Teachers and Training Staff
95	Doctors and Nurses
50	Evangelists and Counsellors

In addition, CBMI maintains a large old people's home in Germany for 75 blind men and women.

Thus, CBMI each year takes care of over three million men, women, and children through its 'Love in Action' ministry, worldwide, with the active involvement of over 200 missionaries and 4,501 national co-workers — doctors, nurses, therapists, dispensers, teachers, rehabilitators, etc.

III

CBMI Commitment

- CBMI is an inter-denominational fellow-ship of committed Christians who are willing to share their knowledge and skills, and also their love and faith with the poorest in the Third World.

- CBMI serves as an international team of experts presenting the whole Gospel to the whole Man all over the world, demonstrating God's Love by word and deed as Jesus did.

- CBMI demonstrates Christian love through practical action, particularly to the needy, the sick and the sightless, to the handicapped, and to the starving people in developing countries, regardless of their race or religion, age or ailment.

- CBMI seeks to enable the national Christians and their missions and churches to build up their social ministries by helping them to run their projects independently and to assume full supervision and responsibility.

- CBMI demonstrates that love is more than words and that Christians from many nations, churches, and denominations are able to work together, fruitfully, through this 'Love in Action' ministry for the welfare and salvation of the poorest of the poor around the world.

All activities of CBMI are based on the firm conviction that millions of people in our ailing world require two things: spiritual guidance, which gives people a meaningful life, and practical help, which relieves the poor from hunger, disease, and ignorance.

Millions of needy people are desperately seeking both.

Since its inception in 1908, CBMI has endeavored to meet these two basic human needs. The physical care provided by CBMI has always been given as a proclamation of God's Love, and the Gospel message has been expressed through practical help as well.

All activities of CBMI are intended to demonstrate that a living faith must manifest itself in works of love.

All CBMI funds are donated by Christians whose main motivation is to preach the Gospel of God's Love and salvation and to demonstrate this love in practical ways.

Thanks to the increasing number of faithful supporters in Europe, North America, and Australia, CBMI has been able to equip its staff members overseas with almost everything they need. The generosity of so many enables its doctors and nurses, its teachers and instructors, to share their skills and knowledge with the poorest of the poor, and to bring about a radical change in their lives. But even more than this, the faithful and active assistance of CBMI supporters from many denominations has enabled our missionaries to share their faith and love with those in need, helping thousands to begin a new life and to find salvation which can only be found in Jesus Christ. Because dear friends of CBMI have demonstrated such a readiness to make sacrifices, they have proven that faith does not merely consist of words, but of deeds as well — Love in Action.

THE CHRISTIAN BLIND MISSION INTERNATIONAL

The Christian Blind Mission International is an interdenominational fellowship of committed Christians who are dedicated to the service of the blind and the handicapped. CBMI follows the "whole" Gospel in order to make men "whole" in the name and for the sake of Jesus Christ.

CBMI seeks to help the national churches by enabling them to extend their witness to God's Love through word and deed.

CBMI's international budget for overseas services is over 40 million dollars which includes administrative overhead of approximately 14%.

If you would like to know more about the work of the Christian Blind Mission International, please write to one of our national offices:

Christian Blind Mission International
International Headquarters
Office address:
Christoffel-Blindenmission e. V.
Nibelungenstrasse 124
D-6140 Bensheim 4, West Germany
Phone: 06251-1310
Telex: 468334 cbmb d

Switzerland, office address:
Christian Blind Mission International
(Christliche Blindenmission International)
Loewenstrasse 40
CH-8023 Zurich
Phone: (01) 2213535

United States, office address:
Christian Blind Mission International
P.O. Box 175
1506 East Roosevelt Road
Wheaton, III. 60189
Phone: (312) 690-0300

Canada, office address:
Christian Blind Mission International
P.O. Box 800
Stouffville Sideroad RR 4
Stouffville, Ontario, L4A, 7Z9
Phone: (416) 640-6464

Australia, office address:
Christian Blind Mission International
P.O. Box 5
1245 Burke Road
Kew, Victoria 3101
Phone: (03) 817-4566

_____

Executive Officers:

Pastor Siegfried Wiesinger,
       International Executive Director

Magdalena Wiesinger,
       President

Guenther Bitzer,
       National Director, U.S.A.

Art Brooker,
       National Director, Canada

Reinhold Gutknecht,
       Interim Director, Australia

For 77 years now, CHRISTIAN BLIND MISSION INTERNATIONAL has tried to help blind and handicapped people through its 'Love in Action' ministry, uniting many thousands of like-minded and active Christians — belonging to many nations and denominations — who are deeply concerned for the physical and spiritual well-being of the neediest people around the world.

The philosophy of our mission is the witness of that faith which is active through love. Today of the 3,968 doctors, teachers, nurses and instructors working for CBMI overseas, 203 are missionaries sent by CBMI from Europe, North America, and Australia.

No needy person seeking help shall be turned away from our door because in every suffering individual we encounter Christ, our brother. Today, CBMI has over 30,000 blind, deaf, physically handicapped, and orphans under its daily care. In addition to that, more than three million eye patients and leprosy victims are helped every year through its medical services.

In our mission, there shall be no religious pressure or discrimination. Today, CBMI's ministries benefit 63 national churches and 90 mission societies around the world.

Our commission is fulfilled only when it is either completed or withdrawn by the One who gave it. Today, CBMI is serving in 98 economically developing countries of the Third World.

CBMI, an independent, international, and interdenominational faith mission, is still financed solely and voluntarily by individuals — friends and supporters — who wish to glorify God by serving the poorest and the neediest around the world.